Images of Our Time

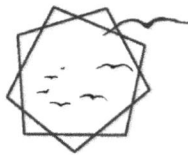

A HISTORY AND PICTURES
OF A PIONEER FAMILY

Images of Our Time

FEATURING THE PHOTOGRAPHY OF
LILLY WILSON CURTIS

TONI GILBERT, MA

WITH

LYLE CURTIS, CONTRIBUTOR

Images of Our Time:
A History and Pictures of a Pioneer Family

ISBN: 978-1-940769-38-7
Publisher: Mercury HeartLink
Albuquerque, New Mexico
Printed in the United States of America

Contact the author at:
Toni Gilbert, RN (Ret.), MA
PO Box 1010
Jefferson, Oregon 97352
toni@tonigilbert.com
www.tonigilbert.com

Mercury HeartLink
www.heartlink.com

To the Ancestors
and ancients
to the family tree
to all who have gone before
and are to come
to our sacred Gaia
our dear Mother Earth
and her generous heart
we send our love
our gratitude
our forgiveness of one another
and of ourselves
We express here and now
our willingness to
be finally worthy
of this great gift
and responsibility
of being the
human form divine
Let us share from across the ages
our most loving
and creative stories of being human
simply because we can

Leigh J McCloskey

ACKNOWLEDGEMENTS

My husband Lewis Judy deserves first place in this list of supportive people that have helped make this book possible. He supports me in my creative endeavors because he understands.

Second place goes to the contributor, Lyle Curtis and to cousins Laurel Christopher Curtis and Nancy Curtis. Without their support and encouragement this book wouldn't have been finished. Then there are the people who are most interested and waiting patiently for the finished product, my brothers Tom and Dan Gilbert. No project would be complete without the many people for whom this work is meant to give pleasure to: my entire family of origin including sisters Terrie, Suzi, and Amelia, my extended family of cousins and my ancestors.

Thanks also go to the talents of Sara Judy for her technical skills, the editor, Jamie Morris and publishing consultant and graphic designer, Stewart Warren.

TABLE OF CONTENTS

ACKNOWLEDGEMENTS   VII

INTRODUCTION   3

Chapter One — 13

OVERVIEW OF THE EARLY NORTHWEST

EARLY OREGON TERRITORY   15

THE NATIVE AMERICANS OF THE PACIFIC NORTHWEST   18

IMMIGRATION TO THE UNITED STATES AND WESTWARD   20

ONWARD TO OREGON   22

WATERWAYS   23

THE RAILROADS   25

THE STAGECOACH   26

Chapter Two — 29

A BRIEF HISTORY OF THE CURTIS FAMILY

A BRIEF HISTORY OF THE CURTIS FAMILY   31

WILLIAM AND GEORGENA WATSON CURTIS   33

A BRIEF HISTORY OF THE CURTIS SIBLINGS   36

SOCIALIZING   45

Chapter Three — 49

THE EMMA MERRICK WILSON LIFE STORY

A Merrick Family Story   58

A Brief History of the Merrick-Wilson Siblings   60

Chapter Four — 71

RUFUS AND LEWIS WILSON CIVIL WAR VETERANS

A Brief History of the Wilson Family   73

Chapter Five — 89

ELLSWORTH AND LILLY WILSON CURTIS HISTORY

Overview   91

Central Oregon   91

Dances in Prineville   105

Freight Wagons   106

Marriage   107

Digging Wells   109

Branding Cattle   112

Crop Harvest   115

Harvesting Wheat   116

Women's Clothing Styles Change   118

Charity Curtis Bowers Memoir   119

Ending a Life Well Lived   158

A Brief History of the Wilson-Curtis Siblings   160

Sources   163

Appendix I
    Documents That Give More Family History   165
Biographies   194

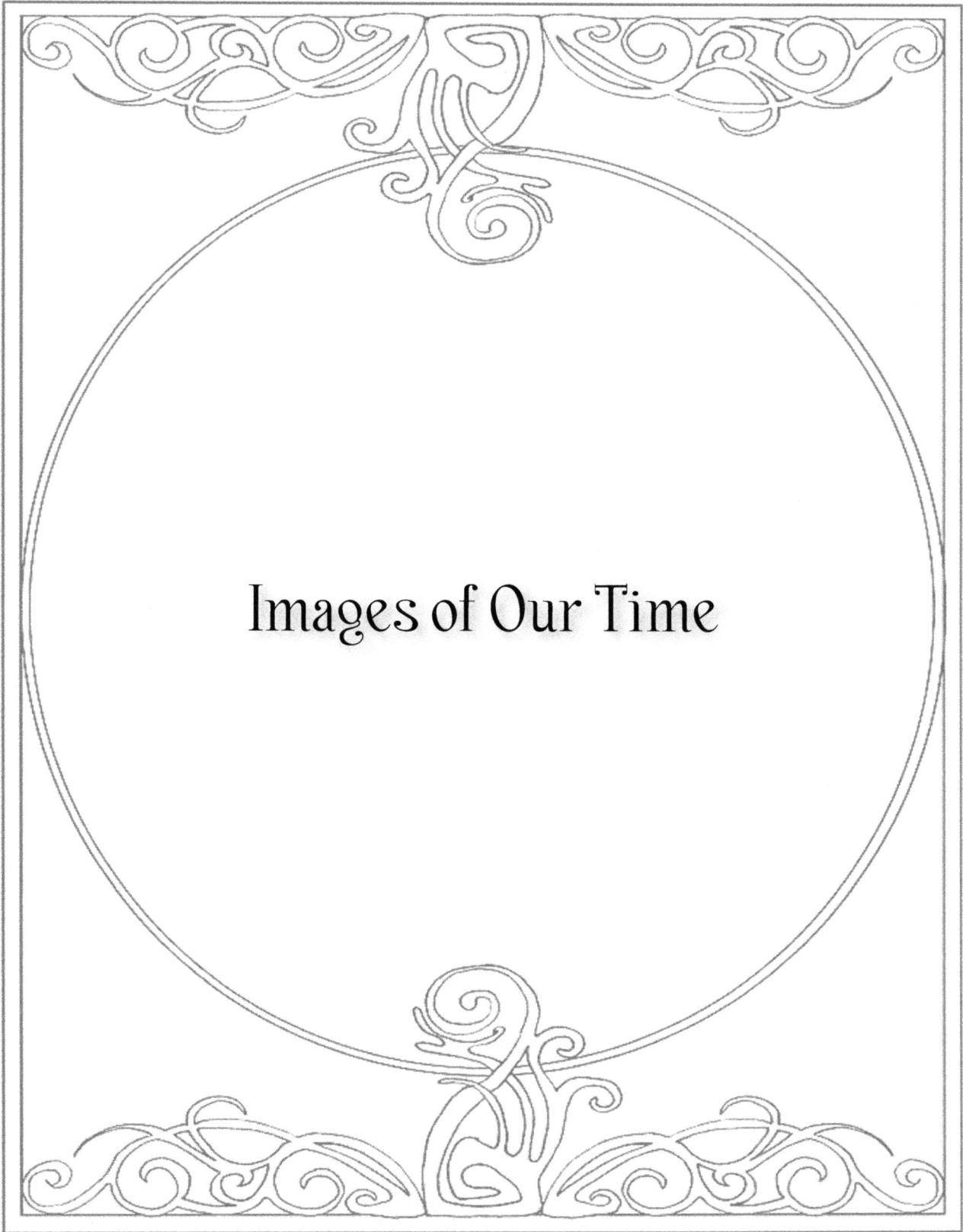

Images of Our Time

INTRODUCTION

In the summer of 2011, my cousin Lyle Curtis organized a family reunion. When Lyle called, I did a quick calculation and surmised it had been over 40 years since I had seen him. Why had it been so long? At one time, Lyle and his family and the entire extended family, were as important to me as my own brothers and sisters.

You can't imagine how excited I was to see Lyle, his wife, Kathy, and his sisters, Nancy and Margaret, as well as all the others, including Don, Dean, and Paul Bowers who agreed to gather in the mountainous area of the Oregon coast, near Logsden, where Lyle, Kathy, Nancy, and Margaret lived.

When I arrived, I saw a bunch of gray-haired people, some of whom had been my childhood playmates. And the white-haired lady in her wheelchair was my mother's sister, Aunt Charity Bowers, who was almost 100 years old. As a preschooler, I spent days and sometimes nights at Aunt Charity's house, near Harrisburg. She had red hair back then. Memory clips of Aunt Charity and everyone else present began playing in my mind.

On the day of the reunion, we met at the site of my Uncle Lewis and Aunt Levona's log cabin. A crumbling foundation and fireplace were all that remained of the pioneer home. But an old Gravenstein apple tree, the fruit of which was a mainstay for many pioneer families, still grew nearby. It was fitting that we shared a potluck meal, conversation, and pictures of our grandparents' time, under this pioneers' tree.

I, myself, had brought the few pictures that had been given to me by our grandmother, Lilly Wilson Curtis. These were photographs that she, first as a young professional, then as a homesteading wife, had taken with her large, wooden-box camera. The negatives were stored on glass plates, which, unfortunately, many plates were later destroyed by

Lewis and Levona Shanks Curtis' log house near Logsten, Oregon.
(Photo Credit: Levona Shanks Curtis)

thoughtless young grandsons with BB guns. The remaining plates are with Lyle Curtis. The prints, however, were stored with several of Grandma Curtis' Oregonian descendants.

At this reunion, I'd intended to share my pictures with the others, especially Lyle. From time to time, Lyle and I had talked by phone about our shared interest in the family history. During the gathering, as Aunt Charity was identifying some of the people in my photographs, my cousin Paul Bowers slipped me a CD with many more pictures—as the thumbnails showed, many were images I hadn't seen before. How exciting was this? Just as it began to dawn on me that I had the skills to put all of this together and create a book, Paul handed me Aunt Charity's handwritten memoir of the homestead years. At the end of her memoir, was a copy of Grandma Curtis's handwritten obituary for her own mother, dated 1946. Now we were cooking; what a treasure trove of pictures and story.

At home, viewing Paul's CD of additional photographs, my eye, refined by education and experience, could see how unique Grandma Curtis's pictures were. At the time she met our grandfather, Ellsworth Curtis, she was a pioneer teacher at a one-room school and owned a photography studio in Prineville, Oregon. After she and Grandfather Curtis married, they homesteaded near Prineville, where they had several children. At times during their years together, Grandma would haul out her huge camera in order to capture images of their homesteading life. Looking through these incredibly precious moments, I began to feel a responsibility to preserve not only her artistic work, but my grandparents' life stories as well.

I sent out a letter telling the cousins about my plan and asking for other photographs. I also began thinking about the things we have learned from the grandparents. How are we putting their teaching into practice in our daily lives? How do those teachings live on through us?

I planned to take about three years writing the text and restoring the hundred-year-old photographs. Also, I needed time to consider the format and message of the book. That time frame would also give my cousins the chance to round up their photographs and anything else that they deemed important to include. As it turned out, I spent three years restoring the old photographs and a year on the text.

In the meantime, Cousin Harold Curtis, who lived in Antelope, Oregon, told me he had another photo album that was given to his father by our grandmother. My daughter, Sara Judy, and I traveled to Harold's house and, with the help of Harold's partner, Betty Samul, began the daunting task of scanning and storing more precious images from the past. I was surprised—and excited—to find even more photographs I had never seen before.

Harold's album also included news clippings of family stories. Several of the newspaper clippings were about Lewis and Rufus Wilson, identical twins, who were Civil War veterans and eyewitnesses to the surrender at the end of the war. It was obvious from the interviews that the twins loved telling their stories.

My brother, Dan Gilbert, loaned me a wonderful little book titled, *A Coon's Tale*. The book was penned by Tom Coon, with the help of his wife, Valda Barnes Coon. This life's work is a collection of short stories transcribed from the oral tradition. After the couple's death, their son, Thomas L. Coon, and daughter, Valda R. Coon, published the short stories. I recognized right away, the cover of *A Coon's Tale* sports a picture of Tom Coon taken by our grandmother, Lilly Wilson Curtis.

Tom Coon and Ellsworth Curtis 1908 (Photo Credit: Lilly Wilson Curtis)

The Coon memoir gives the reader perspective on urban life in the Willamette Valley and Eastern Oregon at the turn of the last century. The book also details accounts of some members of both the Wilson and Curtis families. Ellsworth and Lilly Curtis are mentioned in several places in Coon's book of stories. Tom was an excellent storyteller, and if you listen with your imagination, you can hear his voice in his descriptions of life in the early West.

Throughout history, people have told stories as a way to pass on their knowledge. Important cultural events have been interwoven with personal perspectives, as storytellers expressed what they heard from those living in earlier times and passed on what they witnessed themselves, in their own time. Stories have been transmitted from parent to child, generation after generation, and while some might finally have been recorded, many good stories have been lost to the dust of time's passage because no one was there to listen and pass the tale along.

Grandma Curtis was not only a photographer, she was a storyteller. Many hours of my youth were spent beside her, at the kitchen sink and at the old treadle sewing machine, as she passed on her knowledge, her stories, and her life skills. Twilight hours, when chores were finished, were set aside for reflection, and if you visited her then, she would tell you stories of her youth—stories that were imbedded in the culture of her time.

Grandpa Curtis died when I was young, and I barely knew him, but by all reports he was a gentle, caring person. Grandma lived another twenty years beyond his passing, and was an important part of our family. She set the standards for behaviors for my brothers and sisters and me. She passed on her values both by modeling and by discussing them. I remember her talking to me about truth-telling as we peeled apples at her sink. She taught me to cook, to preserve food for the winter, to sew my own clothes, and to garden. Earlier in her life, she had been a teacher in a one-room schoolhouse and still identified with the role of teacher, correcting my English and—unlike my busy parents, who didn't have time for much of anything other than work and meals—recognizing and encouraging my talents.

Grandma also tried to teach me about men, but I figured she was too old, that her world had been too dissimilar from mine for her advice to apply to me. Needless to say, I believe my life would have been different had I been open to what she had had to teach in that arena. But even so, I was aware that my headstrong grandmother had it together in a way I wanted to emulate. Now, at 60-something, myself, and with grandchildren of my own, her teachings are revealed in similar patterns in my life's story.

In our own time, we pick up the mantle of stewardship; it is up to us to take the traditions we have been given, see what fits with our ideas of how life should be, and continue to honor the traditions of others' lives and times. This chronicle of pioneer lives comprises stories, images, photographs, and historical fact from around the turn of the last century.

The Wilson and Curtis families were descended from Northern European immigrants. They were middle-class pioneers, whose survival depended upon their own hard work. This meant that they arose at dawn and worked until dark, hunting wild game, farming, raising animals, and gardening, ultimately laying the foundation for our current generation and generations yet to come. We can learn about our own lives, both from reading these stories of the past and by gazing into faces of those whose very survival in the world required them to put to full use their abilities and resources.

This book opens, in Chapter One, with an overview of the Pacific Northwest before and during the migration of the Wilson-Curtis family. Chapter Two is a brief Curtis family history. Detailed information uncovered about the matriarchal Merrick branch of the family is given in Chapter Three. The story of twins Lewis and Rufus Wilson, Civil War veterans, is discussed in Chapter Four. And lastly, the Ellsworth and Lilly Wilson Curtis family history and pictures are included, as Lilly's photographs document their lives and times in rural Oregon.

There are approximately 300 photographs in my collection. Ninety percent were taken by Lilly Wilson Curtis, pioneer photographer, teacher, homesteading wife, and mother. Thanks to the legacy of her photographs, the reader gets a glimpse into the dynamics of the Wilson and Curtis families in the context of their culture, its values, fashion, and challenges.

These are stories of people living in a highly uncertain time; the images and personal narratives included portray a life that was indeed demanding, but they also reveal loving relationships and times of fun. The new settlers were not only courageous, but also highly creative. It is difficult to imagine the continuous hard work and many personal losses these men and women endured. Yet, I'm glad they lived as they did, because several generations of their heirs are reaping the benefits of their efforts by enjoying the most luxurious lifestyles in history.

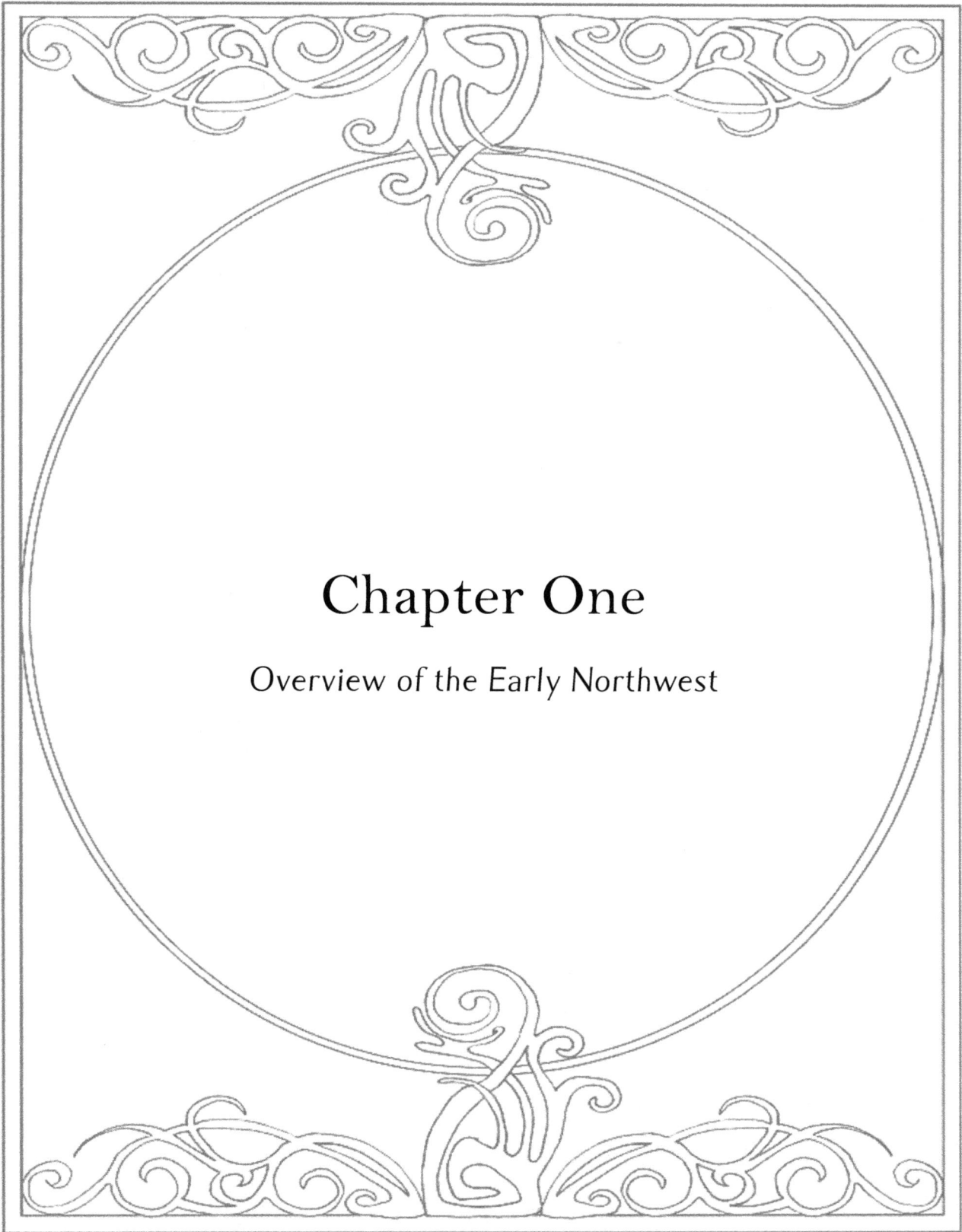

Chapter One

Overview of the Early Northwest

EARLY OREGON TERRITORY

Interest in the Northwest region was first stirred by the search for a northwest passage, a potential water route to East Asia. In search of such a passage, Spanish seamen skirted the Pacific coast from the 16th to the 18th centuries hoping to claim the area surrounding the mouth of the waterway we now call the Columbia River. Englishman Sir Francis Drake sailed along the coast in 1579, possibly as far as Oregon. In 1778, Captain James Cook seeking the award for the discovery of such a northwest passage charted the details of some of the western coastline. At this time, the Russians were pushing southward from posts in Alaska, and the British fur companies were exploring the West. Oregon's furs were an important factor in the expanding China trade, and the Oregon coast was soon active with vessels of several nations engaged in fur trade with the Native Americans. Several British captains, including John Meares and George Vancouver, made the coastal area known, but it was American Robert Gray, who first sailed up the Columbia River in 1792, establishing claim to the areas it drained into.

Canadian traders of the North West Company were approaching the Columbia River country, when the overland Lewis and Clark Expedition arrived in 1805. David Thompson was making his way to the lower river, when agents in the Pacific Fur Company founded Astoria, which was the first permanent settlement in the Oregon territory. That post was sold in 1813 (after the war of 1812) to the North West Company, but in 1818, a treaty provided for ten years of joint rights for the United States and Great Britain in Oregon. This agreement was later extended, and the North West Company merged with the Hudson's Bay Company in 1821, and soon the region was controlled by John McLoughlin at Fort Vancouver.

In 1804, President Thomas Jefferson sent Meriwether Lewis and William Clark, two young army captains from Virginia, on a journey up the Missouri River to travel to the source of the Missouri and then to pass beyond it to the Pacific Ocean. The purpose of this trip was to explore "the most direct and practicable water communication across the continent for the purposes of commerce." The United States had recently obtained the title to this vague territory, called "Louisiana," which stretched from the Mississippi River to the Rocky Mountains.

Jefferson instructed his men to inform the Indian people they met along the way that "henceforward" the Americans would "become their fathers and friends." The goal of the expedition was to study the Native American tribes in the area—as well as the flora, fauna, geology, and terrain of the region. Too, it was hoped the commanders would be able to establish trade with the Native Americans. President Jefferson also wanted to find a direct waterway to the Pacific Ocean so westward expansion would be easier. The expedition was also on a diplomatic mission to transfer power over the lands and the people living there, from France and Spain, to the United States.

On May 21st, 1804, the expedition called the Corps of Discovery, which included Lewis and Clark and thirty-three other men, got underway. Sacagawea, a Shoshone woman, who was married to a French-Canadian trapper, was also part of the entourage. As a twelve-year old, Sacagawea had been stolen from her tribe of origin by a rival band of Indians. Consequently, she spoke more than one Indian dialect, making her an asset to the expedition.

The first part of the trip followed the route of the Missouri River. They passed through places that were to become Kansas City, Missouri, and Omaha. Then, they reached the edge of the Great Plains and saw the area's many different species, most of them new to the explorers. They also met their first peaceful Indians, the Yankton Sioux. Further along on their journey, they had trouble when the Teton Sioux threatened violence if the Corps didn't give them a boat. Both sides prepared to fight, but it was resolved, and the Corps continued up river until winter.

The expedition waited out the winter in the villages of the Mandan Tribe and built Fort Mandan, in present-day North Dakota, where they stayed until April 1805. By this time, they had chronicled 108 plant species and 68 mineral types.

Afterwards, they continued along the route of the Missouri River, until they reached a fork in late May. They were forced to spend time discovering which fork would lead them westward. Then, in June, the expedition crossed the Missouri's headwaters and arrived at the Continental Divide. They were to continue their journey on horseback at Lemhi Pass on the Montana-Idaho border in August. Once over the divide, the Corps took to canoes, traveling first down the Rocky Mountains on northern Idaho's Clearwater River, then down the Snake River, and finally along the Columbia River into present-day Portland, Oregon. The Corps reached the Pacific Ocean in December of 1805, and built Fort Clatsop on the south side of the Columbia River.

They waited out the winter at the fort—and explored the area. They hunted elk and other wildlife, met Native American tribes, and prepared to journey home. In March of 1806, they left, and, upon reaching the Continental Divide, the Corps separated for a short time so Lewis could explore the Marias River, a tributary of the Missouri River. They reunited at the confluence of the Yellowstone and Missouri Rivers in August. The commanders were largely successful, and in the fall of 1806, they returned to St. Louis with journals full of information about the new territory. They ultimately documented over 100 animal species and over 170 plants. They also brought back data on the size, minerals, and geology of the area.

The Indians Lewis and Clark encountered were vital allies on their journey. Entries in the journals of the expedition make it clear there were several moments in the two-year trip when the critical assistance—in the form of food and navigation—provided by the Indians of the Northwest saved the explorers from certain death.

THE NATIVE AMERICANS OF THE PACIFIC NORTHWEST

Archeologists theorize that America's Native Indian history began with the arrival of wandering hunters from Asia, who migrated from southern Siberia to Alaska 14,000 to 20,000 years ago, crossing a frozen land bridge that spanned the current-day Bering Strait—and who then migrated south and began colonizing the New World. This theory has been confirmed by DNA testing.

It is estimated that human habitation of the Pacific Northwest began at least 15,000 years ago, with the oldest evidence found at caves in Fort Rock, Oregon, and the Paisley Caves in Lake County. Archaeologist Luther Cressman dated material from the Fort Rock cave to 13,200 years ago. Scientific excavations and analysis since 2002 have uncovered materials with the oldest DNA evidence of human habitation in North America, in the Paisley Caves in south-central Oregon. This DNA was radiocarbon dated to 14,300.

By 8,000 B.C., the natives had settled throughout what is now the state of Oregon, with populations concentrated along the lower Columbia River, in western valleys, and around coastal estuaries. Archeologists deduce that Indians were probably living in the region when the Romans were building roads and aqueducts in Europe and the Egyptians were building pyramids along the Nile River. These early Oregonian natives may have been established at the time those living in the Tigris Valley in western Asia first began planting crops and harvesting wheat, some 6,000 years ago. Carbon dating of a shallow cave near Oakridge Oregon, in the Cascade mountain range, places Indian presence there 7,000 or 8,000 years ago.

With no written language, early natives passed their history along orally, in mythic stories, presumably, of ancestors, creation, and natural phenomena. What can be known about the early peoples becomes visible when farming, construction, and other earth-moving practices reveal artifacts of their daily lives, such as volcanic glass chipped into arrowheads, bone needles, hammer stones, horn wedges, and shell beads. Archeologists have studied such artifacts to understand how people sheltered themselves from the weather, expressed themselves in art, and aligned themselves with the natural world.

It is very likely that Indians lived along the Cascade foothills on the eastern edge of the Willamette Valley between 6,000 and 8,000 years ago. Artifacts indicate that these people were primarily hunters. About 6,000 years ago, the sites of human activity moved down from the hills to the edges of the Willamette Valley. At this time, Indians dug and baked camas lily bulbs for food and resided in sizable wooden houses arranged around a large central fire pit.

There have been established populations in the Northwest for thousands of years—diverse cultures, complete with distinct languages and traditions, who created connection through commerce, the trading of stories and knowledge, and, sometimes, by making alliances and marriages. Cross-cultural trade meant that items such as Klickitat baskets traveled up and down the Pacific coast. South American feathers were brought to the Northwest, and northwestern shells were carried south. Too, medicines were traded back and forth, expanding many peoples' knowledge of natural pharmacopeias.

A few namesakes of the older nations and their native languages have been retained in Oregon place-names, including, Clackamas, Multnomah, Tillamook, Tualatin, and Willamette. (The Northwest Territory, then

Indian mother and baby taken at the Prineville Studio about 1908. The father didn't want his picture taken. This is the only Indian portrait of the Lilly Wilson Curtis collection.

Oregon Territory, and finally, Oregon, however, are English names of the European settlers.)

Currently, Oregon has nine federally recognized tribes. These are the Burns Paiute Tribe; the Confederated Tribes of Coos, Lower Umpqua, and Siuslaw Indians; the Confederated Tribes of Grand Ronde; the Confederated Tribes of Siletz Indians; the Confederated Tribes of Warm Springs; the Confederated Tribes of Umatilla Indian Reservation; the Coquille Indian Tribe; the Cow Creek Band of Umpqua Indians; and the Klamath Tribes.

IMMIGRATION TO THE UNITED STATES AND WESTWARD

The history of American immigration can be separated into three eras: the Colonial period, the mid-19th century, and the start of the 20th century. Each period brought distinct national groups, races, and ethnicities to the United States. During the 17th century, approximately 400,000 English people immigrated to Colonial America. Over half of all European immigrants to Colonial America during the 17th and 18th centuries arrived as indentured servants. The mid-19th century saw an influx from northern Europe; the early 20th-century, mainly from Southern and Eastern Europe; post-1965 immigrants came mostly from Latin America and Asia.

Historians estimate that fewer than one million immigrants came to the United States from Europe between 1600 and 1799. The 1790 Act limited naturalization to "free white persons"; it was expanded to include blacks in the 1860s, and Asians in the 1950s. In the early years of the United States, fewer than 8,000 people a year immigrated to the new country; these included French refugees from the slave revolt in Haiti. After 1820, immigration gradually increased. From 1836 to 1914, over 30 million Europeans migrated to the United States. Immigrants were predominately male. The journey was dangerous; many got sick, and one in seven travelers died on the transatlantic voyages that carried Europeans to America.

In 1875, the nation passed its first restrictive federal immigration law, the Page Act, which prohibited the entry of immigrants considered to be "undesirable." These included any individual from Asia coming to America to be a forced laborer, any Asian woman who would engage in prostitution, and all people considered to be convicts in their own country. Chinese women were prevented from entering the country even if they were married to Chinese miners and railroad workers who were already here.

By 1910, 13.5 million immigrants were living in the United States. By the 1890s, many Americans, especially those who were well-off, white, and native-born, considered immigration a serious danger to the nation's health and security. Ellis Island was established in 1892, and in 1893, the Immigration Restriction League was formed, which, along with other similar organizations, pressed Congress for severe curtailment of foreign immigration. In 1907, the peak year for European immigration, 1,285,349 persons entered the U.S. through Ellis Island. Congress passed a literacy requirement in 1917 to prevent unskilled, unschooled immigrants from entering the country. In 1921, Congress passed the Emergency Quota Act, which restricted the annual number of immigrants admitted from any country. This was followed by the Immigration Act of 1924, aimed at further limiting the entrance of Southern and Eastern Europeans, especially Jews, Italians, and Slavs, who had begun to enter the country in large numbers in the 1890s.

Immigrants came to America for economic and religious reasons. They left Ireland, Britain, Germany, Denmark, Sweden, and China because landowners forced the tenants out to increase arable acreage; because crop failures created debt and hunger for poor farmers; because factories made products more cheaply than traditional craftsman were able to make them; because religious and political harassment targeted Quakers and Jews; because the German Revolution didn't work out as planned.

The new immigrants swelled the populations of many U.S. cities. Crime burgeoned, housing was often overcrowded, and toilets overflowed, spreading disease. After the expulsion of Native Americans from the South—Kentucky, Tennessee, North Carolina, Missouri and Virginia—many immigrants escaped the worsening urban conditions and resettled in the more rural South. There, they found an economy based on mining, agriculture, and fur trading. And they brought with them a strong, Christian orientation that formed a cultural foundation in these states.

The news got around that west was the direction in which to find fortune and a good life, and the migration spread to the west coasts of the Oregon territory and California. Lewis and Clark described the Northwest's exceptional qualities in their reports, and enough of the tough immigrant population of the fledgling United States responded to these rumors of the wonders of the Northwest to ensure the region's settlement.

ONWARD TO OREGON

Books were written specifically to entice farmers to Oregon. The first overland immigrants to make their way to Oregon with the intention of farming—a small group of 70 pioneers—left Independence, Missouri, in 1841. In 1842, a group of 100 pioneers made the journey from Elm Grove, Missouri. And in 1843, due to a severe depression in the Midwest, combined with a flood of information from fur traders, missionaries, and government officials, all extolling the virtues of the land in Oregon, the number grew to 1,000. These first pioneers followed a 2,000-mile route used by fur traders that took them west along the Platte River through the Rocky Mountains, via the easy South Pass in Wyoming, and then Northwest to the Columbia River. This was to be known as the Oregon Trail. Farmers from Ohio, Illinois, Kentucky, and Tennessee hoped to find better lives at the end of the trail. Even before the Oregon Territory was established in 1846, enormous wagon trains rolled across the prairies in the "great migration" westward. American fur trappers and missionary groups had been living in the region for decades. Trouble between the British that were exploring and trapping in the area and the established American settlers followed. The Americans set out to form their own government, demanding the British be removed from the whole of the Columbia River up to a specified point. War with Britain threatened, but diplomacy prevailed, and in 1846 the boundary was set. However, disagreements over the interpretation of the 1846 treaty were not successfully arbitrated until 1872, in the San Juan Boundary Dispute.

In 1874, two years after that dispute, the Oregon Territory was expanded to include the area west of the Rockies, from the 42nd to the 49th parallel. The area was subsequently reduced to accommodate the creation of the Washington Territory, in 1853.

Oregon was admitted to the Union on February 14, 1859. Founded as a refuge from disputes over slavery, Oregon had a "whites only" clause in its original state constitution. In 1844, Oregon passed laws that prohibited slavery, not out of moral outrage against human chattel, but so that white European politics could effectively exclude blacks and mulattos from the state. A law adopted by the state in 1862 required that all ethnic minorities pay a $5.00 annual tax. In 1923, Idaho, Montana, and Oregon passed alien land laws that prohibited people not eligible for citizenship from owning land, and the following year the Federal Immigration Act denied entry to all Asians. Later laws forbade African Americans from living within the city limits of Portland. Interracial marriage was prohibited by law between 1861 and 1951. Such historical legislation is not only indicative of past attitudes; it is also reflected in the current demographics of rural Oregon, where European Americans continue to be in the majority.

WATERWAYS

The riverways of the Northwest have always been of paramount importance. The indigenous peoples of the region relied on the rivers not only for drinking and washing, but also as sources for the fish—salmon and steelhead—that served as a primary food. Lewis and Clark traveled by river; and when overland routes were carved out for wagons, these were kept close to the rivers so pioneers and other travelers had access to clean water for themselves and their cattle.

To help travelers at river crossings, ferries were established along the important rivers that edged or intersected the Oregon Trail. These included the Missouri River, Kansas River, Little Blue River, Elkhorn River, Loup River, Platte River, South Platte River, North Platte River, Laramie River, Green River, Bear River, Snake River, John Day River, Deschutes River, and the Columbia River. Even many smaller streams boasted ferries. In Oregon, toll bridges were also set up at difficult crossings. While ferries and bridges speeded the journey and helped prevent drowning at river crossings, they also increased the cost of traveling the trail by roughly $30.

In the 1850s, steamboats began to travel the Willamette River. Because these boats couldn't pass Willamette Falls, navigation on the Willamette was divided in two sections: the 27-mile lower stretch from Portland to Oregon City, which allowed connection with the rest of the Columbia River system, and the upper reach, which encompassed most of the Willamette's length. In 1873, the construction of the Willamette Falls Locks bypassed the falls, allowing for easy navigation between the upper and lower river. Each lock chamber measured 210 feet long by 40 feet wide, and was operated manually before the canal was switched to electrical power.

In 1855, the Panama Railroad across the Isthmus of Panama was completed. Paddle-wheel steamships and sailing ships, often heavily subsidized to carry the mail, provided rapid transport to and from the East Coast and New Orleans, Louisiana, to Panama, and then from Panama to ports in California and Oregon. Early settlers sailed up the coast from California to the Columbia River, and then up the Willamette River for a short distance to Portland. The other alternative for getting to Portland was to travel overland by wagon train.

THE RAILROADS

Rail transportation has existed in Oregon, in some form, since 1855. During the last decades of the 1800s, technology and corporations brought advances—as well as exploitation—to Oregon. The state was aligned with the Union states during the Civil War, and a railroad connection was proposed to help supply the Union and build morale. Rail routes were established for a transcontinental railroad that was to operate across the northern tier of the western United States, from Minnesota to the Pacific Coast. Approved by Congress in 1864, construction began in 1870, and the main line opened from the Great Lakes to the Pacific on September 8, 1883.

The influx of settlers to Oregon brought the need for better transportation and better roads. The roads that existed were primitive, deep with mud in winter and choking with dust in summer. There were a number of steamboats on the Columbia and Willamette rivers in the 1850s, but those wanting increased development called for a more comprehensive transportation structure, naming railroads, in particular. It was Ben Holladay who began building the first railroad inside Oregon, the Oregon Central Railroad, in 1869, along the Willamette River, from Portland south for twenty miles. This qualified Holladay for grants, and soon he was able to extend the railroad as far south as Roseburg.

By 1883, the Northern Pacific had created a link with the Oregon Railway and Navigation Company, completing the first Oregon transcontinental connection. A year later, Oregon's Short Line Railroad made a second transcontinental connection to the Union Pacific line in Wyoming, thus branching to the southeast. Eventually, Northern Pacific, Great Northern, and Southern Pacific all served Portland with passenger and freight service.

The railroads helped farmers get goods to other markets. In Linn County alone, the railroad triggered a 250 percent jump in wheat production from 1870 to 1877. The railways carried new and expensive machinery from factories in the East and Midwest to Oregon farmers, who could then become more specialized and make a better profit. As a result, the state grew in manufacturing and diversified in and around agricultural communities. The number of Oregonians working in manufacturing skyrocketed by almost 400 percent in the 1880s. Lumber mills benefited because of the need for railroad ties and trestles. Woolen mills, flour mills, and railroad repair shops often followed the lumber mills. Numerous spur lines carried freight trade farther into previously isolated areas.

When the transcontinental lines were completed, more immigrants from the eastern United States and Europe began arriving in Oregon. Both the Union Pacific and the Northern Pacific railroads sold property along their routes to settlers and others who would eventually need to use the railroads to ship their products. The railroads dispensed countless acres of land at reasonable prices, and Oregon's population grew from 90,000, in 1870, to over 413,000, in 1900.

THE STAGECOACH

Early Oregonians also traveled by stagecoach, a type of four-wheeled, covered wagon used to carry passengers, goods, and mail on an established route and schedule. The

Lilly Wilson Curtis labeled this photograph "My Fast Stagecoach Ride".
The coach apparently ended up with a broken wheel.

stagecoach had strong springs and was generally drawn by four horses or mules. Other vehicles used in the coach line were buckboards, dead-axle wagons, surplus Army ambulances, and celerity (or mud) coaches. Stage-line owners selected the most efficient vehicle based upon the load to be carried, road conditions, and weather.

Widely used before and after the introduction of the railway system, the coaches made regular trips between designated stations, traveling at an average of five miles per hour and covering sixty or seventy miles per day. The term "stage" originally referred to the distance between stations on a route. The coach would travel the entire route in stages, as a fresh team of horses would be waiting at each station, to rest, water, or feed the spent horses. This allowed the coach to continue with no delay. Over time, the word stage came to refer to the coach, itself.

An interesting tidbit from Tom Coon, a one-time stagecoach driver: *During long trips, the coach would stop, at intervals, so the passengers could relieve themselves. The women would head for the bushes on one side of the coach and the men would go in the opposite direction.*

> Ben Holladay, who was born in Kentucky in 1819, moved from Missouri to California in 1852 to operate 2,670 miles of stage lines. In 1861, he won a postal contract to Salt Lake City, Utah, and established the Overland Stage Route. He acquired the Pony Express in 1862. The "Stagecoach King," as he became known, added six more routes and eventually sold them to Wells Fargo, in 1866, for $1.5 million. He built a transportation empire that included steamships and railroads.

By the time of the Lewis and Clark Centennial Exposition in Portland, in 1905, less than 50 years after statehood, the frontier era had passed. Railroads had become the preferred method of travel; most of the feuding on the eastern lands had ended; and cattle and sheep grazed peacefully on fenced-in range. In spring, the fertile Willamette Valley burst with fruit blossoms, and the river cities bustled with trade and industry.

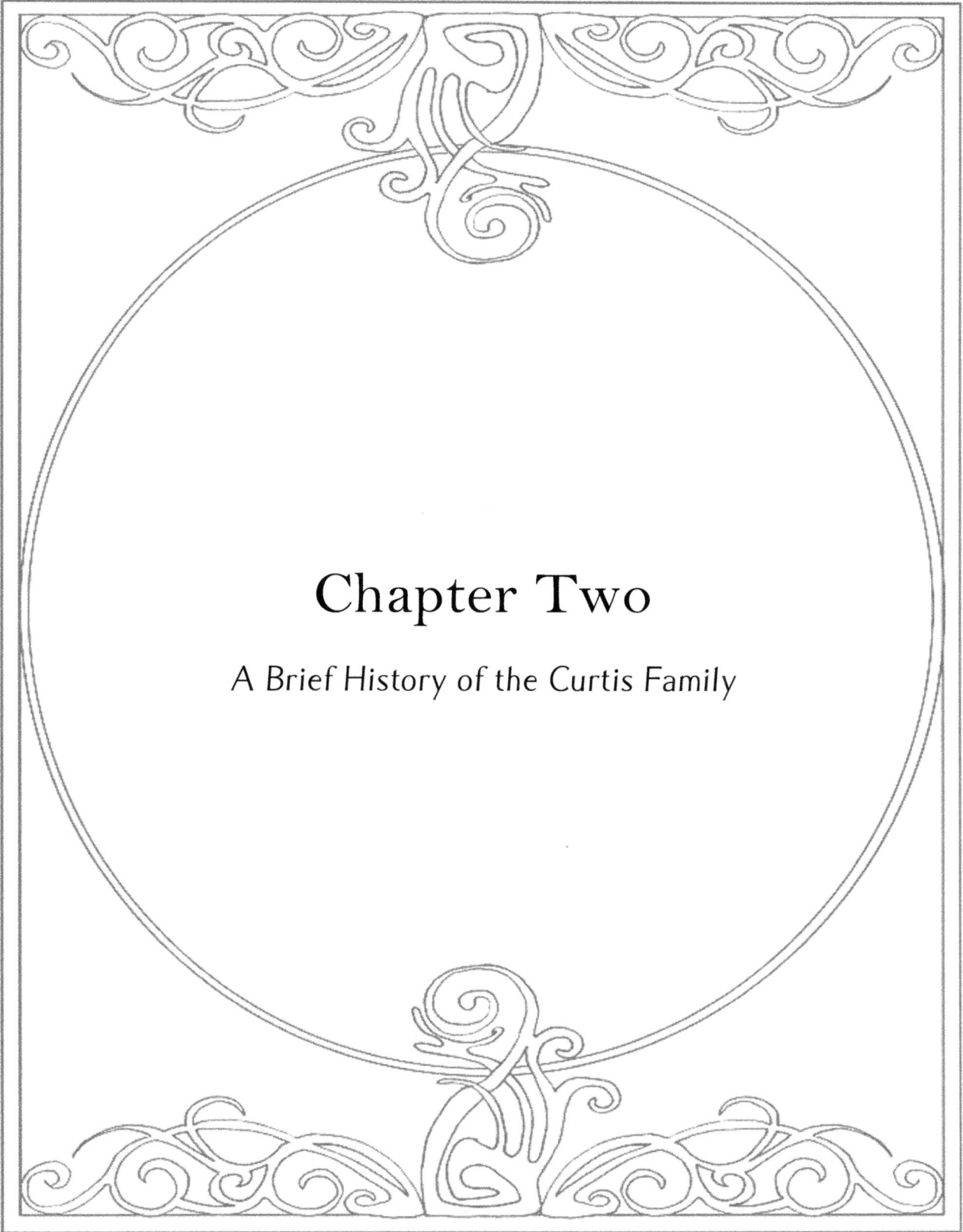

Chapter Two

A Brief History of the Curtis Family

A Brief History of the Curtis Family

After the Lewis and Clark explorations, settlers poured in from many areas of the United States and Europe. Northern Europeans, who comprised the majority of this influx of pioneers, proved the dominant force for further development of the expanding frontier. The Curtis and Wilson families were a part of this wave, immigrating from England, Scotland, and Ireland, some settling in Oregon, after it obtained statehood. Although we cannot know their full stories, what we do know comes from the document collections and memories of their grandchildren.

Joseph Curtis was born in Leeds, Yorkshire, England, on November 26, 1811, the son of Charles and Bettie Brown Curtis. Joseph was the oldest of five children. Upon turning twenty-one, Joseph left Leeds and braved the ocean voyage to America.

Arriving in the United States in 1832, he settled in Oneida County, New York. He married Mary Dickson, daughter of John and Dallie Dickson, in February 1845. Mary, who had been born in England, in May of 1819, eventually bore Joseph seven children: Palmer, Mark, Julia, William, Ellen, Hannah, and John.

Joseph learned the tailor's trade while living in New York. He followed this trade until his fifty-second year, at which time he secured a position in a foundry in Hampton Village, New York. For seven years, he continued this work, and then migrated to Johnson County, Iowa. In 1882, the Curtis family settled on an 80-acre farm of improved land, in Section 29 of Audubon County, in the Greeley Township.

Ten years later, in 1892, Joseph and Mary Curtis moved with their four sons, Palmer, Mark, William, and John, to Oregon, apparently leaving their daughters in Iowa. They traveled by rail to the new port city of Portland. During the trip, women and children rode in the comfortable passenger cars. But the Curtis men, to keep their belongings safe during the long journey, toughed it out in the cold, noisy freight cars. Although little is known about how they traveled once they got to Portland, it was customary to purchase a wagon with horses after the train trip and or hitch a ride with a wagon train. Quite probably traveling the route now known as Highway 99, the Curtis family reached their destination and purchased a farm near Oakville, west of Shedd, a small settlement nestled in the Mid-Willamette Valley, about 80 miles from Portland.

Traveling south on the same roadway, weary travelers would next come to the settlement of Halsey; then to Harrisburg, near the Willamette River and a ferry crossing; and then to Junction City and then to Eugene. The settlements of Brownsville and Crawfordsville were east of Halsey, while both Peoria and Corvallis townships were located a few miles to the west. In time, these small towns would become familiar to the Curtis and Wilson families, as places where they traded goods, purchased supplies, and socialized.

Joseph, Mary, and their four sons were farmers. Mark and Palmer had prune orchards, with dryers to dry the prunes. The Curtis family also grew corn and wheat. Too, family history indicates Joseph adhered strongly to the principles of the Democratic Party.

Tom Coon, who was a neighbor of the family, mentions three of the Curtis brothers in *A Coon's Tale*. He notes that his own family was poor, and the Curtis brothers, who had more assets, set up a contract with Coon's father for the Coon boys to cut wood near John Curtis' home for $1.50 a cord. They fell, bucked, and split the wood in four-foot lengths, then stacked it in a straight line, four feet wide by eight feet long, a configuration known as a "cord." Tom Coon also tells how Mark and Palmer Curtis built a washing machine, first constructing a tub with legs and wooden slats, then building a half-circle tub with slots that fit into slots in the top of the tub, arranging it so it wouldn't hit the slats in the bottom. This contraption had a round stick extending upright from its center. When the tub was filled with water, the handle was used to rock it back and forth.

Joseph and Mary are buried, along with their sons Mark and Palmer and Palmer's wife, in the Oakville Cemetery in Linn County, Oregon.

WILLIAM AND GEORGENA WATSON CURTIS

William Curtis (Mary and Joseph Curtis's third son) was born in Oneida County, New York, on July 14, 1856. William attended school in his youth, continuing his studies when, the year he was ten, the family moved to Iowa. He remained with his parents until he was twenty-four and married Georgena (sometimes spelled, "Georgina") Watson, second daughter of Thomas and Mary A. Howe Watson. Georgena was born in Princetown, Bureau County, Illinois, on June 20, 1861. Georgena's parents were of Scottish and Irish descent. Like William's parents, Mary and Joseph Curtis, Georgena's parents arrived in New York, and then moved to Illinois, and when Georgena was two years old, on to Johnson County, Iowa. There, Georgena attended school until she was eighteen and became both a musician and an accomplished horsewoman, who took much pride in riding and training horses. After they married, William and Georgena spent a year in

William and Georgena Watson Curtis on their 50ᵗʰ wedding anniversary
(Photo Credit Lilly Wilson Curtis)

Johnson County, Iowa. In the spring of 1881, they moved to Audubon County, Iowa, and settled on a farm of 240 acres, all fenced and under cultivation. William and Georgena made many improvements on the place and were successful in raising and handling livestock, especially sheep and cattle. According to a family document, they had "a well-stocked farm as the result of industry, thrift, and wise management."

When William and Georgena moved to Oregon in 1892, William's parents and his three brothers Palmer, Mark, and John were with them. Georgena left all her relatives in Iowa. Their first home was near Shedd, where a baby girl, Ethel, the Curtis's seventh child, was born—just three weeks after the family arrived in Oregon. They moved again to acreage near Peoria, and still later, to a plot of land four miles north of Harrisburg, near Alford Railroad Station and Cemetery.

Then, in 1910, William and Georgena moved to Olds, Alberta, Canada, to a 480-acre ranch where they engaged in mixed farming. They were following the custom of buying a property, making improvements, then turning a profit. With that profit, another property

Curtis family and home, located near Alford Station

Curtis family portrait, bottom row: William, Charity, Georgena, and Florence, second row: Ellsworth, Seymour, Alice, and Ethel Back row: Dale Chester and Jay

Curtis home in Canada

Barn near the home in Canada (Photo Credit unknown)

would be purchased. Ideally, each subsequent farm purchased would be bigger than the last.

In 1919, William and Georgena returned to Oregon, settling around Lebanon, then, in 1935 they moved to Halsey. Georgena passed in 1937 and William in 1940. They are buried at Alford Cemetery outside of Harrisburg Oregon.

A BRIEF HISTORY OF THE CURTIS SIBLINGS

CHARITY CURTIS (1882-1952)

Charity was the twin to Ellsworth, and they were the first children born to William and Georgena. Ellsworth was older by a few minutes. Charity attended school at Greenback, near Oakville. Later, she finished her schooling in Harrisburg, residing with the Pryor family. At that time, she became a member of the Christian church.

In July of 1902, Charity married Roy Willoughby. They had one son, DeLos. When DeLos was several years old, Roy died of a ruptured appendix.

Charity and Ellsworth Curtis (rear) aprox 1888. (Photo Credit unknown)

In 1908, Charity married her second husband, Bert Clark. They returned to Iowa with DeLos. A daughter, Georgena, was born to them. They moved to Olds, Alberta, Canada, about 1912, but were there only a short time. Due to Charity's health problems, they returned to Oregon in 1914 and went into business in Halsey. According to family documents, Charity was active in the Christian Church, was a member of the Rebekah Lodge, and was a leader of 4-H sewing clubs. She was always doing something for someone, sewing or baking or anything else her limited means permitted. She died at Sacred Heart Hospital, in Eugene, on February 28, 1952.

ELLSWORTH THOMAS CURTIS
(SEE ELLSWORTH AND LILLY WILSON CURTIS, CHAPTER 5.)

Charity Curtis and second husband Bert Clark

SEYMOUR JOSEPH CURTIS (1884-1946)

Bert Clark and Seymour Curtis

Seymour Curtis

Seymour lived at Alford Station, until his marriage to Arzalea McClain. They moved to Canada about 1910, settling on a ranch at Olds, Alberta, an English community, where tea was a tradition. They had tea and angel food cake for "tea time." Word has it that Arzalea was a wonderful angel food cake maker. Their only children, two infant sons, both died at birth. Seymour farmed for many years and, living so far north, "had the different experience," according to the Velda Curtis Kropf memoirs, "of having light almost all night in the summer."

Canadians by choice, Seymour and Arzalea visited Oregon a short time before Seymour passed away, on April 15, 1948. He is buried in Alford Cemetery, in Harrisburg, Oregon. Arzalea lived her last years in a retirement section of a hospital in Trail, British Columbia.

CHESTER ARTHUR CURTIS (1886-1948)

Chester stayed with Uncle John (Jack) and Jennie Curtis, who had no children of their own. Chester attended Grasshopper, Greenback, and Oakville Schools. He credited his Uncle Jack for encouraging his interest in arithmetic, a subject in which he excelled. Uncle Jack and Chester slept in adjoining rooms and, before school, while they were both still in bed, they talked back and forth through the thin wall, Jack drilling Chester on the times tables.

Chester worked for his uncle Jack for room and board while in school. He arose at daybreak and cut wood with an old crosscut saw until about 8:45, then left for school, which was a mile away. As soon as school was out, he hurried back home to cut more wood; he worked until dusk and supper time. Chester repeated this routine year after year, and when Jack passed away, he willed Chester the biggest share of his estate, north of Harrisburg, which amounted to several thousand dollars.

Then, at twenty-one years old, Chester went to Prineville to find employment. He ended up driving a team of horses in a wagon train over the mountains, a journey that took seven days. Chester also drove a stagecoach, which was pulled by four to six horses, and for which he was paid $40.00 a month, with room and board. His first stagecoach route was between Prineville and Rosland (now LaPine). They stopped first in Bend, 35 miles from Prineville, before continuing on to onto LaPine. Later, he drove between Prineville and Shaniko.

Chester loved horses and owned many in his lifetime. Once, bringing a horse home from Eastern Oregon, he rode to Portland, and then he and the horse boarded the steamship to make the trip up the Willamette River to Harrisburg. While aboard the ship, he bent to scoop a bucket of water from the river for his horse. Something made him look behind him, where he saw a man standing poised to hit him over the head. However, when Chester looked at him, the stranger withdrew his advances and walked away. Chester thought the man probably wanted his horse—as it was a pretty one—and planned to throw him in the river after hitting him.

In 1909, Chester married Della Tandy, a daughter of Charles and Clara Goodlin Tandy, pioneers in the Junction City area. Charles was the son of Edwin Napper Tandy, a judge of Lane and Linn counties.

Chester went to Canada in 1911, but came back in 1912. Chester and Della's first home in Oregon was north of Harrisburg (probably the estate he inherited from his uncle Jack). They then moved to Rowland, east of Harrisburg. According to Floyd Mullen's book, *Land of Linn*, Chester planted some oats. They grew well, but his crop was contaminated by another grass. He cleaned the oats in a fanning mill and saved the queer-looking seed. He sent a sample to the Portland Seed Company, which he asked them to identify. They said the contaminating seed was Italian (annual) ryegrass, and they would pay him seven cents per pound for all he could grow.

From 1916 to 1944, Chester lived at Alford Station, in the house his parents had lived in before they moved to Canada. About 1926, Chester built a service station on his property at Alford, and then built a new home on Muddy Creek in 1946. Chester became director of Muddy Creek Irrigation, was a school-board member for years, and served on other boards at different times, as well. He raised horses and had a wild, roan stallion named Ladd. His workhorses were beautiful. His favorites were a team of matched roans named Florence and Dorothy.

According to family, Chester had many friends, loved being around his grandchildren, and spent many hours visiting. Tom Coon related that, in later years, Chester had a "severe operation." When Chester was finally able to go see him, Tom reported, *we had the finest visit two people could ever have. We spent the day together and laid plans for the future. He had a duck pond on his ranch, and the boys had a certain day to shoot, so we had our day planned. He knew I was a rock hound, and he had a few big rocks in his field, and no one could figure out how they got there. I was to go over and make tests of them to find out if they were meteors. We had a big laugh and said, if they were, we had our fortune made, but we never got together again before he passed away.*

FLORENCE CURTIS BROCK (1888-1960)

The Curtis family moved to Canada when Florence was 22 years old. Henry Brock, then 26, went to Canada to get Florence. On the way back, they were married at Calgary by a Methodist minister.

The Brock's first home was about four miles west of Halsey. While a young bride, Florence became very ill. Dr. Dale of Harrisburg was called, and he put her on the kitchen table and operated immediately. The surgery saved Florence's life, but there is no mention of what the ailment might have been. The couple was unable to have children, so it may have been a female problem, such as a tubal pregnancy. Still, Florence and Henry loved children and kept others' children in their home. They eventually adopted an infant, Doris, and raised her as their own.

Florence sewed for nieces and great-nieces and, in her lifetime, helped many people in other ways. Henry was a fine horseman and immaculate in his dress and surroundings. He always had a beautiful horse and buggy, and his home and farm were showplaces.

Florence and Henry Brock lived at Alford Station, for a number of years. Florence liked to tell the story of her brothers bringing an Eastern Oregon coyote pup home for a pet. The animal was tied up because he was very wild and would eat chickens, and they were fearful for the safety of their younger brother, Dale, who wanted to play with the coyote. The family lived near Southern Pacific Railroad, and trainmen became familiar with the coyote as they stopped to switch trains. They knew of the family's concerns and, one day, told the family to box the animal up, and they would take him to the Portland Zoo. On their way to Canada a few years later, Florence and Henry saw the coyote pacing back and forth in his cage at the zoo.

The Brocks sold the farm in 1940 and moved to a house on River Road, in Eugene. There, Henry worked at odd jobs, until his death in 1958. Florence lived out her remaining years in a retirement home in Junction City.

JAY HARLAND CURTIS (1890-1954)

As a young man, Jay Curtis lived in Canada and Linn County and worked on farms. In 1915, he married Ida Hogue, who lived near Harrisburg. After their marriage, they went to Canada and lived with William and Georgena and the younger members of the Curtis family.

The first home of Ida and Jay was west of Lebanon. It was there that Jay began farming. Later, the couple moved to another farm, south of there, and later still, to a larger farm to the southeast. That farm had timber, as well as more acreage. A horse was necessary to round up the sheep for dipping and shearing and to bring the cows in to be milked. Jay liked horses more than any other stock and enjoyed horseback riding. The first team of horses he bought, after marrying Ida, was named Bill and Jim. He brought them to Oregon, when they moved from Canada, around 1920. On the train, Jay rode in the boxcar with the horses, making sure they were taken care of.

Apparently, the family rented that larger farm, because the Kropf documents state, "During the 1930s, the landlord had to give up this large place, so the family [Jay's] moved nearer to Lebanon to a much smaller farm." Jay and Ida eventually moved into the town of Lebanon, where Jay bought a logging truck and began hauling logs. The couple had three daughters: Marjorie, Florence, and Charlotte. In 1941, Jay became the road supervisor for Linn County, and, as his district began in Brownsville, he was required to live there. He bought six acres and built a barn for his saddle horse, Strip, so named because of a white strip down his nose. Jay was also a member of the Calapooia

Roundup, which was held in Crawfordsville every year.

ETHEL EDITH CURTIS (1892-1979)

Ethel Curtis aprox 1920

Ethel spent her childhood four miles north of Harrisburg, across from the Alford Cemetery. As an adult, she took training from Dr. Dale of the Harrisburg Hospital and became a nurse, a good one. During the 1918 flu epidemic, she helped many people, and she also made sure her relatives received good care during their times of illness.

Ethel married Charles Poole, and had one son, Curtis Poole. Charles owned a funeral home in Brownsville. The Pooles later moved the funeral home to Eugene, under the name of Poole-Larsen Funeral Home. In her later years, Ethel owned and operated

Bathurst Lodge, at the coast. As an elder, she lived first in an apartment in Junction City and, later, in a Eugene nursing home, where she passed away.

ALICE MARIE CURTIS (1895-1980)

As a child, Alice went to a country school in Alberta, Canada, and helped on the family farm. She enjoyed herding sheep and cattle with her horse, and kept the coyotes away. She liked to ice skate on a lake near their home and loved country dances. She attended Olds Agriculture College.

Alice married Bob Allen in 1914 and moved to Vanscoy, Saskatchewan, Canada, where her new husband had a homestead. Their three children, Erwin, Ethel, and Seymour, were born at the homestead, where they farmed the land and underwent many hardships. The family drove a sleigh to town for groceries during snowy Canadian winters; then, in 1925, they moved to Oregon and lived through the Depression. Bob got work where he could, sometimes earning a dollar a day. After Bob passed away in 1958, Alice married Otto Thompson, in 1960.

DEAN CURTIS (1901-1918)

Born in Shedd, Oregon, Dean was the next-to-last child of William and Georgena. He was named after Dean McWilliam, who operated a store in Halsey.

As a child, Dean, lived with his family four miles north of Harrisburg and in 1918, when he was nine years old, the family moved to Canada. The flu was a serious epidemic at that time, in both the United States and Canada. It took the lives of many people, in 1918, Dean was among them.

DALE WILLIAM WATSON CURTIS (1907-UNKNOWN)

Dale was born near Harrisburg (Alford Station), where he lived until he was three years old, when his parents moved the family to Olds, Alberta, Canada. Family documents tell a story about Dale, shortly after the family's arrival in Canada. In the States, he had been accustomed to buying a nickel's worth of jellybeans. But in Canada, when he asked at the store for a nickel's worth of "beans," he was given shelled beans to cook. Upon his return home, he said, "These Canadians don't know beans from candy."

Dale attended Mowers School, near his home in Canada, through the fourth grade. After the family moved back to Oregon, he attended both elementary and high school. In 1920, his parents purchased a home in Lebanon, at 1092 Williams St., where they lived until 1935, when they moved to Halsey. Dale remained in the Lebanon family home.

Dale married Elizabeth (Betty) Mae Alvin on June 28, 1936, in Lebanon. They had one son, Michael Dale Curtis.

SOCIALIZING

Members of this pioneering generation found picnicking a fine way to socialize. Families agreed to a meet at a designated picnic spot, at a given time—usually in a grove of trees and on a Sunday. One such picnic grew into an annual tradition: People came from all over to attend the several-days-long event known as the Brownsville Picnic—an event which continues to this day.

Brownsville, a small town in the southern Willamette Valley, was founded in the 1840s. It is conveniently located within 25 miles of Eugene, Albany, Corvallis, Sweet Home, and Lebanon. The 26-acre Brownsville Pioneer Park has been in use since the town's inception. Bordered on two sides by the Calapooia River, it offers summer swimming and was a wonderful spot for winter-weary pioneers looking for a few days relief from their hard working lives.

The Curtis and Wilson clans, along with their friend Tom Coon and his family, looked forward to the Brownsville Picnic and attended every year. Tom said he and his brothers *would shine our horses up with a curry comb, and brush and tie a sack of grain or oats on the back of our saddle, take a lunch with us, and stay all day. It is interesting just how much money father divided between four of us. Sometimes we would have 25 cents, sometimes 30, and never more than 50. We could buy balls to throw at the nigger babies for one penny each, so each of us would buy five, and the fun would start. These stands just had a canvas about ten feet high for a back stop, and we would throw one of these balls at the wooden doll, then throw the next ones over the canvas into the brush. The operator would try to stop us, but we had bought the balls and could throw them whenever we pleased, but the next time we came to throw them he would say no sale. He had us branded.*

Coon goes on to describe the merry-go-round that cost five cents to ride, as did the Ocean Wave. *The Ocean Wave was supposed to perform like a wave on the ocean; the operator would instruct the riders to stay apart, and when he got us all spotted and away we went; when it got in full speed, we all ran together, and the dirt would fly; he stopped as soon as he could and kicked us off, so we couldn't do any business there with him either.*

The picnic also brought in new concepts and inventions to demonstrate to a future market. Tom described hearing recorded music for the first time: *We noticed some people standing in a circle with something stuck in their ears, with an insulated wire running into a box. This cost ten cents, so we invested a dime, and it sure was something. It was music from a phonograph concealed in a box. People were all excited over this.*

As the picnic wound down, the excited Coon boys found ways to entertain themselves. *By now, 25 cents of our money was gone, so the next thing was a sack of popcorn for five cents. That cleaned us out of money, and we wanted to ride the merry-go-round some more, so we would stand around and wait 'til it was under way, and when the ticket man had his back to us, we would grab a horse by the neck and go for a ride; when he came to get the ticket, we would search our pockets, and while one of us was doing this, the others would mount a horse, so all of us would have a free ride. This would only work about twice, and then the fun would be over. The picnic would last about four days, if I remember correctly, but we were only good for one day because of lack of money.*

Today, Brownsville Pioneer Park boasts ball fields, horseshoe pits, a dining pavilion, and a covered amphitheater. These amenities complement downtown Brownsville's wonderful 1880s-1920s commercial buildings, as well as the town's many historic houses, some of which date back to the 1850s.

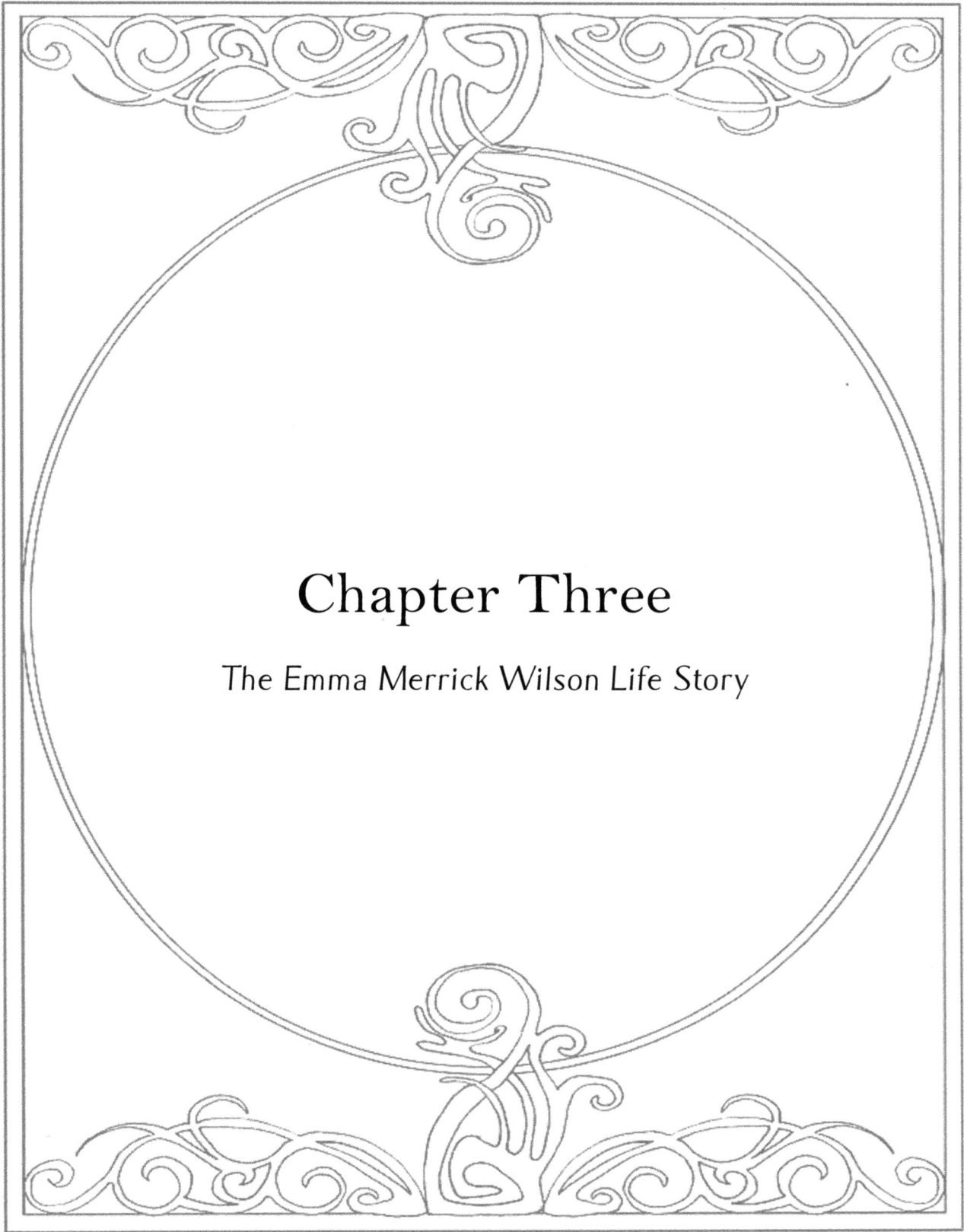

Chapter Three

The Emma Merrick Wilson Life Story

Emma Merrick was born on September 2, 1849, near Vermont, Illinois, where her parents were pioneers. Her father was Morris Merrick, and her mother was Jane Hankins. Jane Hankins was born and raised in Virginia, Illinois, and lived near the home of Nancy Hanks, the mother of Abraham Lincoln. In a newspaper interview, Emma said she was a relative of Nancy Hanks, although a sister disputed this claim in a letter. Although Emma regarded herself as Irish, her patriarchal lineage can be traced back to John Merrick, born in 1654, in Herefordshire, England.

When Emma Merrick was sixteen years old, she married Lewis Ramsey Wilson, aged 24. Apparently, they hit some rough times because, after her first baby was born, Emma moved back to her parents' home. The whole story isn't known, but what is known is that Emma's father told her that she was married and should return to her husband. Was Emma's marriage a happy one? Was it abusive? We don't know, as there are few clues to the type of relationship she and Lewis had.

Later, Lewis and Emma Wilson, as well as Emma's parents, Morris and Jane Hankins Merrick, left Illinois and traveled eleven days by covered wagon, heading for the newly settled country of Iowa, eventually making their home in the scattered settlement of Audubon, near Des Moines. The Wilsons lived in Waukee, Iowa, for several years, where Emma's ten children—Curtis, Clarence, Alwilda, Bert, Nellie, Morris, Lilly, Abby, Erman, and Blanche—were born.

During the period she had children at home, Emma remained a dutiful farm wife. Her daily chores included tending a flock of chickens. The family would use what chickens they needed for meat and eggs and, it wasn't unusual for someone to stop by to purchase a chicken for their own family.

Emma cooked on a wood stove in the kitchen and had another stove outside for canning and cooking during the hot summer months. She made her own bread and jams, grew an asparagus bed, and cultivated large dandelions for winter greens. Everyone in the family

Wilson Children 1887 Back row: Clarence, Alrvilda, Bert, Abbie, Lilly, Morris, Erman, and Blanch. (Photo Credit unknown)

arose at the crack of day and went to bed at dark. The hours in between were spent working at tasks that ensured their survival through the next winter. But Sunday was a day of rest—for everyone except the women, who made the meals for the day. Emma's daughter Lilly would later tell her grandchildren that Emma was "a good, hard-working woman, who was neat and tidy."

After the Wilson's Iowa farm was improved, according to an interview with Emma, the grasshopper plague struck. The hoppers devoured everything in their path, making a wasteland of fertile fields and gardens. The grasshopper horde proved too much for the Wilsons: they left Iowa for Oregon. Emma's mother died in Iowa, but Emma's father, Morris, accompanied Emma and Lewis on the move west. Later, Emma would say that when the family left Iowa, the grasshoppers were so thick the sun was dimmed by the massive, moving insect cloud.

The Wilsons arrived in Portland on the first Northern Pacific train to reach that city after the railroad was finished. Once there, Emma welcomed four of her sisters to Oregon: Martha Merrick Standard, whose Oregon address remains unknown, Lillie Merrick Hathaway and Mary Merrick Gibson, who both lived in Eugene, and Fanny Merrick Gray, who lived in Salem.

Emma Wilson, Martha Standard, Mary Gibson, Fanny Gray and Lillie Hathaway 1910
(Photo credit: Churchley, Portland, Oregon)

Lillie Hathaway, who arrived in Oregon in 1880, came from Iowa, via San Francisco, by train, continuing north on a steamer to Portland. She later reminisced, in a newspaper interview: *There wasn't a single bridge across the river when I arrived in Portland, and practically everywhere we went, we had to travel on foot. Two ferries were operating there at the time, one at Larson Street and the other at the railroad station.*

Blanche G. Merrick, another of Emma Wilson's sisters, never left Industry, Illinois. She married John N. Janes, in 1893, and had a son (whose name remains unavailable) and a daughter, Beatrice. John Janes made a living as a toy manufacturer and restaurateur.

Emma also had three brothers: John, Charles, and George. All three fought on the Union side during the Civil war. Her father also joined, but was too old for the fighting. Instead, he worked as a nurse, helping wounded soldiers and organizing a hospital for Company 1 of the 62 Illinois Infantry.

Not much is known about Emma's brothers, but this story was uncovered in a newspaper article: In an interview by Lucy Lenora Andrews, Emma Wilson tells how her brother, Charles Merrick, then but a boy, enlisted in the Union Army at the beginning of the Civil War. For some months during the war, Merrick was incarcerated in the Anderson prison, where he subsisted on cracked or parched corn until he became so weak that, when released, he could hardly walk. Not yet 19 years old, he came home on furlough almost a living skeleton, bent and walking with a cane. However, he regained his health and returned, only to be killed in his regiment's last engagement, which was the last battle in North Carolina at the end of the struggle.

In the book *The Pursuit of Hoke's Division*, Captain Herman Lund, commander of the 16th Illinois, Vandever's brigade, which was Charles Merrick's unit, describes part of the battle: *We were met by a withering fire of musketry and canister from six guns, which the enemy had in position on our left flank... The men were completely exhausted by marching at double-quick so long and our line was confused, broken, and disorganized... The left of my regiment was within thirty yards of the rebel breastwork, from which we were receiving a most destructive fire...upon our left flank, while another line was pouring it into us directly in front. At this time all of the Fourteenth Michigan on my right had fallen back, and I deemed it the wisest course to withdraw the regiment from such a position as speedily as possible.*

The Wilson family, with Morris Merrick accompanying them, traveled by overland wagon train from Portland to McMinnville, Oregon, and, from there, looked over advertisements for land. In 1885, they bought property and settled on a ranch near Halsey, at a place called Nixon Station, in Linn County, Oregon. Nixon Station was where the railroad stopped to pick up goods and foods, such as milk and wheat, to deliver to towns farther down the line.

Emma and Lewis's children attended school at Lake Creek, riding their ponies back and forth from the schoolhouse, until a school building was constructed nearer their home. While it was customary, in some families, not to educate women, the Wilsons insisted all their children, including the girls, get an education.

When the Oregon Electric Railroad laid tracks through the ranch at Nixon Station property, the Wilson's house was relocated to the other side of the tracks from the barn, orchard, and the water well. After the railroad moved the house, in 1905, the Wilsons built a one-story addition onto the house.

The Wilsons built another barn, using only joinery and wooden pegs, and made other improvements on the farm, which they owned for 40 years. The house and barn were removed in the 1970s, but the property is currently owned by a great-grandson. The property became an Oregon Century Farm in 1985.

According to an oral account, the aging Lewis Wilson sold the family's ranch at Nixon Station to Lilly and her husband, Ellsworth Curtis. It may be that he didn't discuss the sale with his wife and daughters, as, in those days, a woman didn't have the right to own property or even have rights to her children and so Lewis was able to do as he wished. Some of the details of the sale have been lost, but the story has it that, in 1928, Clarence Wilson, a friend named Robert Montgomery, and two of the Wilson daughters were living on the farm, when Lewis returned from Prineville. There was some sort of disagreement—even, possibly, a physical encounter—between those living on the farm and Lewis. Soon after, he showed up at Lilly's home near the Wilson ranch with a scratched up hand that was shut in a gate. Subsequently, Lewis had the four evicted (see document in the appendix), after which, Clarence took Lewis to court claiming he was insane. However, when the court date arrived, neither Clarence nor any of the others made an appearance, and Lewis was able to convince the judge he was of sound mind and could make good judgments.

A newspaper article states, "Before her husband's death, Mr. and Mrs. Wilson observed their golden wedding anniversary on their farm, and each year since his death, a family reunion has been held on the anniversary date." Unfortunately, according to Lilly's storytelling, the rest of the family, including Emma, didn't see or speak to Lewis or Lilly again after the farm was sold to Lilly and Ellsworth. The deal was that one of the children would purchase the farm and pay the rest of the family, which is what Lilly and Ellsworth did. We can speculate that either the price or something about the way the transaction was handled, may have figured in the dispute.

So which story is the true one? Did they meet once a year at the Halsey farm, as the newspaper article reports? Or did they not see each other after the dispute? Lilly said that Emma lived in Prineville until 1931. After surgery for appendicitis, she lived with her daughters, Abby and Blanche. Abby and Blanche lived out their lives in Portland, less than a hundred miles from Lilly's home. However, none of Lilly's grandchildren ever met Emma, Abby, or Blanche; such a meeting was never presented as an option. Lilly wasn't given to telling tall tales, and as far as Lilly's family knew, she wasn't speaking to her sisters or her mother. Lilly openly talked of the dispute and told her family that, after the controversy over the ranch, Emma and Lewis never saw each other again. Emma's character is not fully known. She did pass on a few other stories that could be either wishful storytelling or authentic oral histories of family events. We will never know which. Granddaughter Charity Bowers remembered her grandparent's relationship, before the dispute, as "congenial." At the time that she knew them, they were older and had separate bedrooms.

It may help us to understand the situation if we view it in terms of the culture of the time: Emma's world was a man's world. The prevailing patriarchy assumed male privilege over women's freedom. Not only did women have no rights to own property, they had no rights to their own children. No language existed to discuss marital rape or domestic violence, and women were even denied credit.

Women of the era rarely had both a family and a career. Although a few women physicians practiced medicine, rather than being addressed as "Doctor," they were called Miss or Mrs., depending upon their marital status. And it was typical, when a woman married, for her to become pregnant soon after the marriage and, thus, even more dependent on the men in her family. In Emma's case, she and Lewis had ten children, five of whom died from diseases of the day, leaving only five to survive into adulthood. Her lot must have seemed a burden of gigantic proportions. Perhaps this is why she advised her surviving children not to marry, encouraging her daughters to have careers instead—which is exactly what Lilly, Alwilda, and Abby Wilson did, although Lilly and Blanche ended up marrying.

The suffragettes' movement in the late 19th and early 20th centuries was the first wave of feminism, a movement that eventually won American women the right to vote. Emma heartily agreed with the movement, and, unlike of many of her contemporaries, made sure her daughters were educated and had an understanding of the affairs and politics of the times. And Lilly, while not taking part in any of the suffrage demonstrations, also supported the cause.

Because news traveled slowly in those days, suffrage, like all political and social reform, did not progress quickly. It took another wave of feminism, in the 1960s, to liberate women to the point of today's freedoms.

A Merrick Family Story

Lyle Curtis traced the Merrick family line back several generations, to 1654, in Hereford-shire, England. He uncovered one interesting story in a document titled, "The History of Bucks County, Pennsylvania, Chapter XL, Bucks County in the Revolution, 1774 to1783, from the discovery of the Delaware to the present time by W. W. H. Davis." On page 6, the document states that, in preparation for the crossing of the Delaware and the Battle of Trenton, George Washington and his officers, Greene, Knox, and Hamilton stayed in several homes and mansions near the Delaware River—including the Merrick house: "A fourth of a mile away across the fields, on the road from Newton to Neeley's mill, is a stone dwelling, 20 feet square, with a kitchen at the west end, and the farm was bought by Samuel Merrick in 1773 and now [in 1905] belongs to Edward, his descendant. When Green occupied it, the first floor was divided into three rooms, now all thrown into one, and the family lived in the kitchen. As the house was recently built, and not yet finished, the general had the walls of the room he occupied tastefully painted, with a picture of the rising sun over the fireplace. At this time Samuel Merrick had a family of half-gown children about him, who were deeply impressed with passing events, and whose descendants are full of traditions of the time. Greene purchased the confidence of his [Merrick's] young daughter, Hannah, by the gift of a small tea canister, which was kept in the family many years.

The Rhode Island blacksmith [who was part of Washington's company] lived on the fat of the land, while quartered with this Upper Makefield farmer, devouring his flock of turkeys and monopolizing his only fresh cow, besides eating her calf. In return he allowed the family to use sugar from the barrel bought for his own mess. At the last supper before Trenton, when Washington was the guest of Greene, the daughter Hannah waited upon the table, and kept the plate from which he ate as a memento of the occasion.

The document goes on to describe the other homes and the people present when Washington's officers and troops sought shelter and comfort during the American Revolution. On page 7 of the document, it states, "Washington rode over to Merrick's and took supper with Greene, the evening of December 24th, and no doubt Knox, Sterling, and Sullivan were there. The family was sent across the fields to spend the night at a neighbor's, so there would be no listeners to the council of war that destroyed the British Empire in America.

A number of families living in the area remained loyal to the English and, at the end of the war, were punished by losing their homes. Some of the estates were valuable; one such estate contained 1,412 acres. The government sold the homes and made a sizable profit.

A BRIEF HISTORY OF THE MERRICK-WILSON SIBLINGS

CURTIS WILSON(1867-1888)

Curtis Wilson died of pneumonia at 21years old.

CLARENCE WILSON(1870-1945)

Clarence Wilson lived and worked with his parents, helping with the ranch at Halsey. He also had a homestead in Prineville.

[left] Clarence Wilson 34 years old

[right] Awilda (Affie), Lilly, Blanch, and Abby 1908 (Photo Credit: Lilly Wilson Curtis)

ALWILDA WILSON (1872-1948)

Alwida never married. She taught at the first public school in Redmond, situated in the old hardware building in 1907 and sponsored a school program to raise money to buy the first school bell. The unexpected highlight of the program came when the butterfly costume of one of the young performers caught fire from the lamps. (The child remained uninjured.) Alwida also taught in Culver and Prineville, until 1912, when she moved to Albany and taught there until 1928. She moved to Portland in 1928 and is buried in Pine Grove Cemetery, near Halsey.

BERT WILSON (1874-1924)

Bert Wilson also lived and worked with his parents at the Halsey ranch and had a homestead in Prineville. He died of polio at age 50.

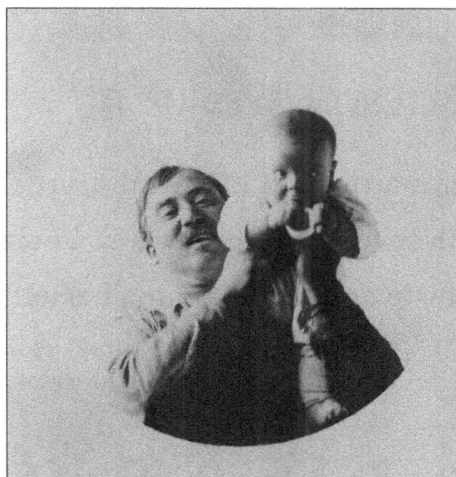

*Bert Wilson with
baby Lewis Curtis, 1913*

NELLIE WILSON 1876-UNKNOWN)

Although Nellie's date of death is unknown, she probably died in childhood.

MORRIS WILSON (1878-1898)

Morris Wilson died from complications of measles and pneumonia at 20 years old

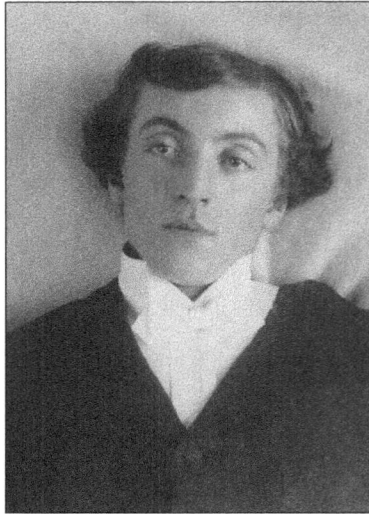

Unusual picture in that he appears to be lying down and his eyes are hooded. As was the custom of the day, this may have been a death-bed picture of Morris Wilson.
(Photo Credit: unknown)

LILLY WILSON (1882-1974)

Until her marriage to Ellsworth Curtis, Lilly was a teacher and photographer. She bore Ellsworth seven children, two of whom were stillborn. She lived to see five of her children grow to adulthood, dying, herself, in old age.

Lilly Wilson high school graduation from South Public School 1900 (Photo Credit: unknown)

ABBY WILSON (1884-1962)

Abby never married.

Abby Wilson (Photo Credit: Lilly Wilson Curtis)

Abby Wilson (Photo Credit: Lilly Wilson Curtis)

ERMAN WILSON (1887-1906)

Erman Wilson died of typhoid fever at 18 years old.

Erman Wilson

Erman Wilson 17 years old

Erman Wilson 18 years old
(Photo Credits Lilly Wilson Curtis)

BLANCHE WILSON HYDE (1889-UNKNOWN)

According to records in the book *Remembering Schools Days of old Crook County*, Blanche was a teacher in the Lower McKay, in 1814. The school was located four miles north of Prineville. She married L. A. McFadden. The couple lived in Redmond, where Blanche taught seventh grade. Blanche's father-in-law was Dr. E. O. Hyde of Prineville.

Blanch Wilson 18 years old
(Photo Credit: Lilly Wilson Curtis)

Blanch Wilson, 1907
(Photo Credit: Lilly Wilson Curtis)

Emma Wilson with grandchildren Lewis and Charity Curtis 1917
(Photo Credit: Lilly Wilson Curtis)

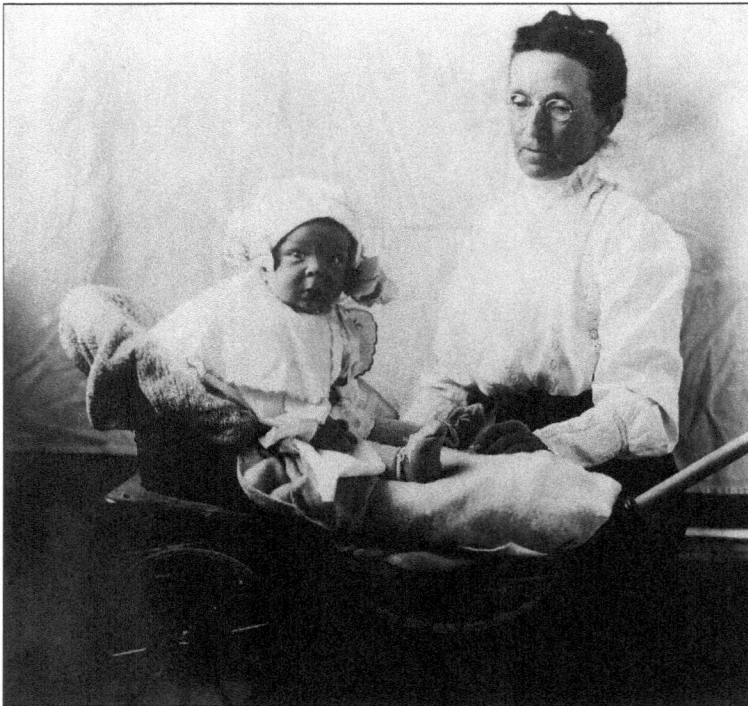

[Clockwise from top letf] Blanch and Emma Wilson, 1903; Emma Wilson with Lewis and Charity Curtis 1917; Emma Wilson (L) at 90 years old and sister; Emma Wilson and baby Lewis Curtis 1913. (Photo Credits: Lilly Wilson Curtis)

Chapter Four

Rufus and Lewis Wilson Civil War Veterans

A BRIEF HISTORY OF THE WILSON FAMILY

Lawrence Delanto Wilhelm (1857-1934), son of Suzana Wilson (a sister of Lewis and Rufus Wilson), was a schoolteacher with a penchant for genealogy. Lawrence spent a good deal of time and money researching the Wilson family lineage. According to his account, he garnered information from four main sources: his early ancestors' documents; other family records; his observations; and historical and court records. Currently, Lawrence Wilhelm's records are in the keeping of Lyle Curtis.

The Wilhelm records state that he obtained the history of the Wilson name through the Research Bureau in Washington, D.C. He learned that "Wilson" is an Anglo-Saxon name, which descends from a prince of Denmark, prior to 1000 A.D. Descendants of that first Wilson family settled in England, Scotland, Ireland, Wales, and France. The surname "Wilson" is patronymic: it's derived from a personal ancestor whose family name was "Will," whose sons were called "Will's sons," which was eventually rendered as "Wilson."

There are many distinct lines of Wilsons throughout Europe and America. Over the course of history, Wilsons have been prominent as barristers, authors, artists, and scientists. In Europe, Wilsons have been knights, baronets, and members of parliament; and, in America, they've been generals, captains, and members of congress—with one Wilson serving as a president of the United States.

A continuous record of the branch of the Wilson family under consideration, here, begins in the 14th century. John Wilson, whose great-grandfather was the "Will" of the original Wilsons relevant to this Wilson history, settled in Bradfield, England, in 1369. Later, a descendent, Thomas Wilson (1564-c.1658-1630) settled in Sterling, Sterlingshire, Scotland, and took part in the battle of Boyne, for which services England gave him 1,800 acres of land in the north of Scotland. Hugh Wilson, son of this Thomas Wilson, came to America in 1726, settled in Eastern Pennsylvania, and laid out the town of Easton, Pennsylvania. He served in the French and Indian Wars, and his grandsons served in the Continental Army.

William Wilson, also a part of this line of Wilsons, came from Ulster, Ireland, in 1732. He settled on 200 acres six miles from Philadelphia. His sons, Thomas and William, both served in the Revolutionary War. The offspring of this branch of the family migrated to Virginia and Tennessee and are purported to be the ancestors of the Wilsons discussed in this book.

Hugh Wilson, Sr. (1780-1847), was born in Williamson County, near Franklin, Tennessee. Records state that he was a roving character. Truly a pioneer, Hugh could not endure living in a wholly civilized community. He was such a lover of Indians that, when the creation of settlements where he was living sent resident Indians looking for new territory, he followed their tribes. His wife, Susan Skiles (1782-1857), was as delighted to be on the move as he. She said the food tasted better [when they were moving].

Hugh Wilson moved from Tennessee to Indiana Territory, in 1814. Then, after a year or two, he moved on to Christian County, Kentucky, and from there to Arkansas. Although Hugh wanted to go further south, upon his family's objections, he moved, instead, to Wayne County, Missouri, and from there to Schuyler County, Missouri, in 1825. Then, in the fall of 1826, Hugh Wilson moved to McDonough County, near Carter's Settlement, near Industry, Illinois. In the spring of 1827, he headed toward Des Moines Rapids, in Lee County, Iowa. But when he neared the town of Webster, in Hancock County, he met brothers-in-laws William Job, William Southworth, and Ephram Perkins. They persuaded him to go to Job's Settlement, where he settled on Section 9, in Hire Township. Here he erected a "half-faced camp," which was just a hog shed enclosed on three sides and open to the south.

After raising a crop, Hugh built himself a more substantial residence. But about two weeks after he moved in, a friendly Indian came to the cabin and told him that a marauding band of Indians was on its way, and he had better leave. Taking the Indian's word, he moved his family keeping just far enough behind the Indians to be out of danger. Next, he settled in Des Moines Rapids, where he secured a large tract of land.

Hugh disliked living in town, saying he would just as soon go to the penitentiary. He died at the age of 67—a death attributed to his grief at the fact that his children would not go west with him to the new state of Colorado. Hugh Wilson is buried in the Wilson Cemetery, upon a big bluff on his own farm. His wife, Susan, died at the age of 75 and is buried in the Wilson Cemetery near Fort Madison, Iowa.

Next in the lineage is John Wilson (November 2, 1806-January 18, 1886), father of Lewis and Rufus Wilson, Civil War veterans. John Wilson was born in Jackson County, Tennessee and moved with his father, Hugh Wilson, Sr., to Indiana Territory, then to Christian County, Kentucky, and then to Wayne County Missouri, and, in 1825, to Schuyler County, Illinois. In the spring of 1827, John moved again with his father, this time, to McDonough County, and then, to Hancock County, Illinois. In the fall of 1827, to avoid an Indian raid, John moved with his father, Hugh, to Fort Madison, Iowa. He returned to McDonough County in 1828. That same year he married Martha R. Vance, who was born in Tennessee, on May 11, 1809. She was the daughter of James Vance, Sr., who came from Tennessee in 1826 and was the third white man to settle in McDonough County.

Hugh Wilson and Susan Skiles Wilson had the following nine children:

Amaranth Wilson (dates unknown) married while her father lived in Missouri and died there before her father moved to Illinois. She bore one child, but it is not known whether that child lived; the name of Amaranth's husband is unknown, as well.

Sarah Wilson (1803-1867) married Richard Dunn. The following children were born to them: Richard Dunn (who wed Martha Barclay); Pharon Dunn, who died on February 13, 1850; Thomas Dunn (who wed Evaline Barclay); John Dunn (who wed

Nancy Jewell); Newton Dunn (who wed Marie Jewell); Jasper Dunn; Jolin Dunn; James Dunn; George Dunn; Susan Dunn; and Anna Dunn (who married three husbands, Werly Crook, James Bullard, and E. B. Warton, bearing three sons for Werly Crook). Both Sarah Wilson Dunn and Richard Dunn are buried in the Wilson Cemetery near Fort Madison, Iowa.

John Wilson (November 2, 1806-January 18, 1886)

George Wilson (July 22, 1809-March 20, 1891)

Thomas Wilson (1815-April 2, 1870)

James Wilson (September 4, 1816-April 14, 1886)

Mary Wilson (dates unknown)

Daniel Wilson (April 11, 1826-September 12, 1884)

William Wilson (dates unknown)

Married in 1828

John and Martha Vance Wilson, the first couple married in what was later to become McDonough county. The picture, the original of which is in the possession of their grandson, L. D. Wilhelm of Macomb, was taken about the time they celebrated their fiftieth wedding anniversary on Oct. 30, 1878.

John and Martha Vance Wilson, 1828

John and Martha Wilson were the first couple married in McDonough County. The ceremony was performed by Reverend John Logan, a pioneer Baptist minister. When John and Martha set off on their wedding tour—a trip, on horseback, to visit John's father, Hugh, near Fort Madison, Iowa—

their journey took them along an Indian trail through the woods and over the prairies. They passed only one house before reaching Hugh's home.

In 1829, John and Martha built the first log cabin on Section 23, of Industry Township, Illinois, where they resided for a number of years, raising a family of twelve children— six boys and six girls— all of whom John and Martha saw married and settled in their own homes.

Then, in 1854, John and Martha built what was considered a "very commodious" and up-to-date frame house, where they spent their declining years in comfort. Martha died in that home near Industry, Illinois, on April 26, 1881, and John died in the same home on January 18, 1886. They are both buried in the Vance Cemetery.

John and Martha Vance Wilson home in Illinois where Lewis and Rufus grew to adulthood. Built in 1852 of Black walnut and plywood, this picture taken approx. 1930 when the structure was in decline. (Photo Credit: Lilly Wilson Curtis)

John Wilson and Martha Vance Wilson had the following twelve children:

Elizabeth A. Wilson (August 2, 1829-July 22, 1857)

Mary V. Wilson (October 1, 1830-April 5, 1908)

Hugh Wilson Jr. (April 4, 1832-January 16, 1912)

Sarah Wilson (October 7, 1833-November 9, 1891)

James V. Wilson (December 11, 1835-May 23, 1921)

Susana A. Wilson (April 24, 1837-December 29, 1864)

William V. Wilson (September 6, 1838-February 19, 1908)

Christopher Wilson (December 25, 1839-September 9, 1915)

Lewis R. Wilson, twin (October 26, 1841-November 1, 1931)

Rufus R. Wilson, twin (October 26, 1841-January 20, 1935)

Margaret R. Wilson (June 29, 1843-January 30, 1881)

Martha R. Wilson (March 17, 1845-February, 1904)

LEWIS AND RUFUS WILSON

Twins Lewis and Rufus Wilson, Civil War veterans, were born to John Wilson and Martha Vance Wilson on October 26, 1841. Lewis Wilson married Emma Merrick. Their story is told in Chapter 3.

The following photos credit: Lilly Wilson Curtis

Rufus and Mary (L) Emma and Lewis (R) Wilson, 1908

MR. AND MRS. R. R. WILSON

Mary and Rufus Wilson, 1908

Lewis Wilson with Civil War metal approx. 1930; Lewis, Martha (Tiny) Curtis, and Rufus Wilson, 1931; Rufus and Lewis Wilson, 1932

Rufus Wilson (L) Martha Curtis on rock, and Lewis Wilson, 1931; Lewis Wilson with baby Martha and Pat Curtis 1927

Lewis and Emma Wilson with grandchildren (L to R) Lewis, baby Morris and Charity Curtis, 1918; Lewis and Rufus Wilson in 1930. One could tell the twins apart in picture because Lewis' wife Emma was a fastidious person and kept his clothes neater than Rufus' wife kept his clothes.

Lewis Wilson with his namesake Lewis Curtis, 1913; Charity, Emma, Lewis W. and Lewis C. with baby Morris, 1918; Rufus and Lewis Wilson with unidentified sons approx. 1910

The following Civil War stories are from newspaper articles (see Appendix). Because the references have been removed, it is impossible to tell the source. However, since Lewis Wilson lived in Linn County, Oregon, the interviews may well have been published in an Albany paper. At that time, nearing 90 years old, they were touted as being the oldest surviving Civil War soldiers.

During one interview, the journalist writes, Exchange of banter is the chief diversion of these two brothers, whose lives have been more closely interwoven than those of most kin. In reference to Lewis moving to Oregon, while Rufus stayed in Iowa, the interviewer asks Rufus, Why did you finally separate?

"They wouldn't let Lewis stay at Waukee," Rufus said, smilingly.

"I wanted more adventure, but Rufus showed the white feather," Lewis retorted.

The interviewer writes, "And so they talk, pausing now and then to live over again their long and eventful lives."

Both Lewis and Rufus Wilson voted emphatically in favor of the notion that Sherman was right. "It sure was hell," Rufus said. Neither of the veterans relishes recollections

Rufus and Lewis visiting on the back porch steps (Photo Credits: Lilly Wilson Curtis);
Rufus and Lewis Wilson, 1905 (Photo Credit unknown)

of the dark side of the war. While they escaped harm themselves, they parry questions about the shot and shell phase of their service. Even when exchanging reminiscences with each other alone, they dwell upon their pranks and youthful escapades, rather than upon their achievements at arms. No boasting passes their lips.

"I'll never forget the day I discovered I was a sprinter," Lewis said. He alluded to a time when his infantry regiment was attacked by rebel cavalrymen. "We had orders to retreat, and I sure obeyed them," Lewis recounted. "We raced to a swamp, where they couldn't follow us, but it seemed to me I was standing still until I realized I had outstripped those horses. I guess I was about the fastest man in our regiment that day."

"Where were you all this time?" Rufus was asked.

"Right ahead of Lewis," Rufus replied.

Lewis and Rufus Wilson fought for three years against the Confederacy without receiving a wound. They fought in so many engagements that they became discouraged when they tried to count the battles. They fought side-by-side for more than two years. They joined Company 1, 8th Illinois Regiment, in August 1862, and were not "mustered out" until early in 1865. They lacked but two months of being 21 years old when they enlisted. Not until General Sherman and his army reached Atlanta, GA., and Rufus was assigned to an ammunition wagon, were they ever separated. Even then, they remained members of the same regiment.

The Wilson twins were born in Industry, in McDonough County, Illinois. The brothers, members of a large family, grew into young manhood at their parents' home and answered the call of patriotism as soon as they were of age. They returned, after the war, to Industry, but a few years later Rufus moved to Iowa, settling on a farm at Waukee, near Des Moines. Bonds of brotherhood would not be broken, so Lewis soon followed his comrade and kin, establishing himself a home adjacent to Rufus. Both grew corn there, until Lewis again heard a call. It was that of the West. So, in February of 1885, he packed up his household goods and came to Oregon. He lived on a farm near Halsey.

Rufus visited Lewis in Oregon in 1930, at the time of the newspaper interview. Lewis went to see Rufus in Iowa twice, and to attend Grand Army of the Republic conventions that were nearby. The Grand Army of the Republic conventions were fraternal organizations composed of veterans of the Union Army and the Union Navy, Marines, and the U.S. Revenue Cutter Service, who served in the Civil War. The conventions linked men through their experience of the war and became the first advocacy group in American politics, supporting voting rights for black veterans, promoting patriotic education, and helping to make Memorial Day a national holiday. The Grand Army of the Republic also lobbied the United States Congress to establish regular veterans' pensions and supported Republican candidates. At its peak, in 1890, The Grand Army had more than 490,000 members.

According to a newspaper article, Lewis and Rufus enlisted together in the Union Army in 1862. They told their companies that they hailed from "the devil's half acre,"

McDonough County, Illinois. "Before long the boys knew we were telling the truth, for we were two of the meanest in the company," they said.

They had been in skirmishes by the score and at least a dozen battles. Quincy, Illinois, was their training camp under the direction of Capt. G. H. Runnels. From Quincy they marched to Louisville, then to Nashville and Franklin, Tennessee. They had no actual battles, until the three-day fight at Chickamauga, Sept. 18, 19, and 20, in 1863. After that it was Mission Ridge and Lookout Mountain. They were also a part of Sherman's famous march to the sea.

"We had one good meal on that march," they said. "Twelve of us went out and foraged for our meal. Then we cooked it. We expected to wake up and find ourselves dead after that stuffing."

During the war, the two were always together, feeling a responsibility to one another. It was at Chickamauga, Tennessee, that the twins saw their first action, and it was in this battle that they came nearest to death. The two were standing side-by-side during the battle, when a bullet passed directly in front of Lewis and passed through Rufus's trousers, near his belt line. "My pants were nearly torn off, but the bullet never touched my skin," Rufus said.

From then on, the Wilsons were in many campaigns and saw much hand-to-hand fighting under several commanders. They were with General Sherman's army on its march through the South. At Atlanta, Rufus was detailed to drive an ordinance wagon, but this service remained no less dangerous than was that of Lewis, who remained with Company 1. "Often he was compelled to drive through storms of shot and shell." Rufus said. "But neither he nor his wagon was ever hit.

Lewis related one of his many contacts with death: While he and other officers and men of his company were standing near a campfire in North Carolina, just before the end of the war, a Confederate detachment opened fire on the regiment. Wilson's captain was struck by a cannon ball and was hurled into the flames. Lewis seized the body and pulled it from the fire, but to no avail—the captain was dead.

The Wilsons were identical twins. Their commander's adjutant officer discovered only after a year that there were two Wilsons in Company 1, and then only when he came upon the two together when inspecting their arms as they were about to go upon guard duty.

Promiscuous foraging, whenever detected, involved penalties, the Wilsons said, but they recalled with glee one occasion on which they, among others, escaped, though they were caught. Members of a party, including the twins, had stolen a chicken apiece with one extra. They had cooked the fowls with corn meal seasoned with stolen salt. They had each eaten a chicken, saving the extra one for the captain in anticipation of possible detection.

Sure enough, the following morning, the captain lined up his company and commanded the foragers to step forward. So many men obeyed and stepped forward, that the officer was puzzled. "Take your positions," he finally said. "I haven't enough men to guard you, so there's no use arresting you."

Lewis sold a "taken" hog and, at the time of the newspaper interview, still had some ten-cent pieces as part of the proceeds from the sale of the hog that he took from a southern farm. Years later he gave the dimes to his granddaughter Charity Curtis Bowers.

As the newspaper reports, Both brothers were at Richmond when Lee surrendered, and it was Lewis's privilege to see Jefferson Davis, disguised in his wife's clothing, brought out from hiding by federal officers.

Rufus and Lewis Wilson were mustered out as privates at Washington, D. C. and imme-

diately went back to Illinois. Both had been offered chevrons during their army careers, but neither would accept.

Lewis Wilson and Morris Merrick, both Civil War Veterans, are buried at Pine Grove, and their gravestones indicate their patriotism. It is an interesting experience standing at the foot of those who have seen so much and, now, see no more.

Rufus Wilson in his woodlot at 90 years old,

At this Wilson Family Reunion the youngest at the table was 89 years old.
(Photo Credits: Lilly Wilson Curtis)

Pine Grove Cemetery, west of Halsey, Oregon, is one of the many pioneer cemeteries in Linn County. In addition to being the final resting place of many early pioneering men, women, and children, it is also distinguished by the graves of several soldiers. It is one of many pioneer cemeteries in Oregon that have historical value. You can see that at least one of the ancient soldiers fought in the Indian Wars because the headstones indicate war, name, rank, and division.

http://www.linncountyroots.com/Cemeteries/PineGrove.htm

Driving Directions to Pine Grove Cemetery:

From Highway 34, between Corvallis and Albany, go south on Peoria Rd. about 11 miles to Pine Grove Road. Turn west to the cemetery and chapel.

From Halsey, go 4.5 miles west on American Drive on to Peoria Road. Then go 0.3 miles and turn west on Pine Grove Road.

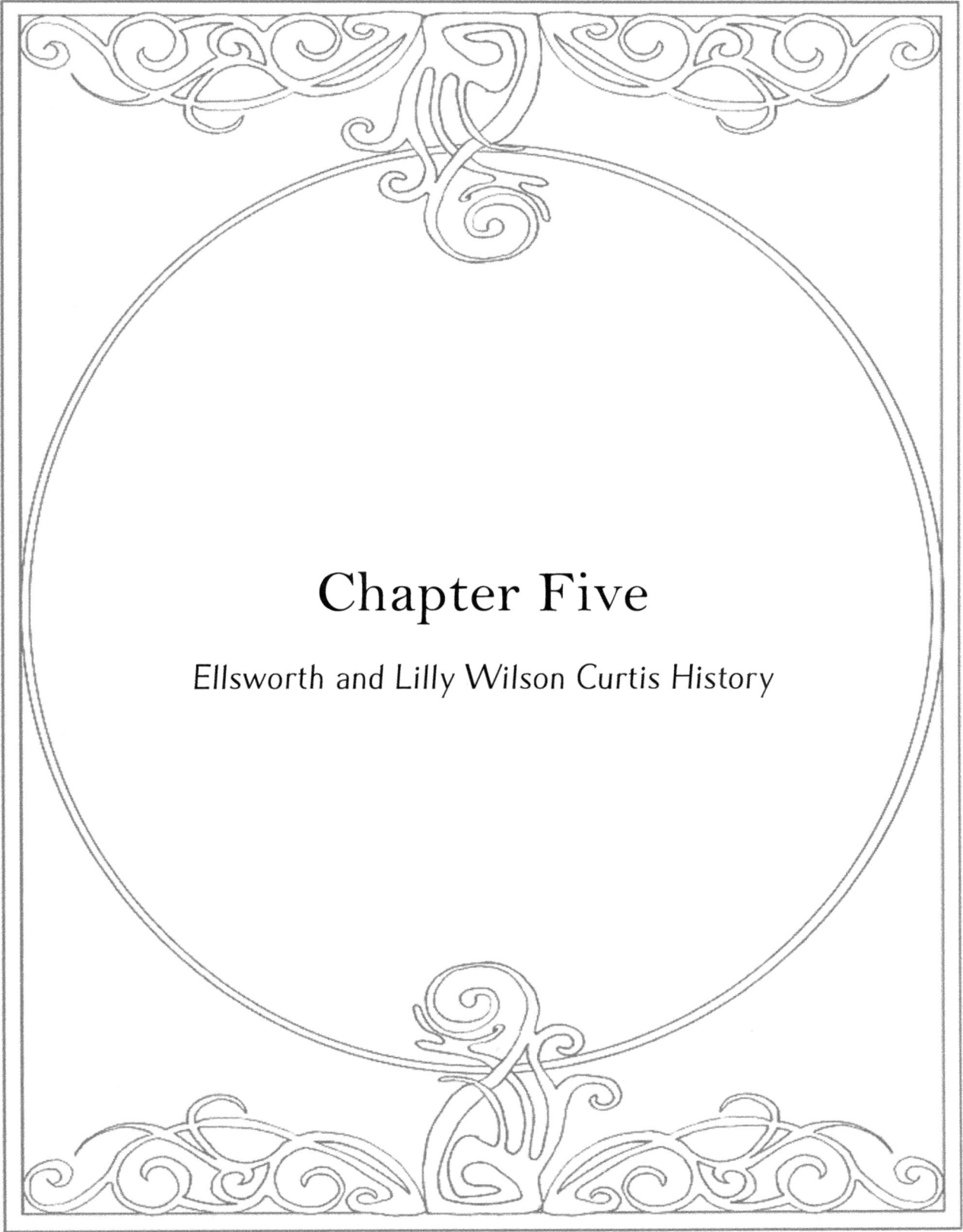

Chapter Five

Ellsworth and Lilly Wilson Curtis History

Ellsworth and his twin, Charity, were born in Iowa, in 1882, the first children of William and Georgena Watson Curtis. The family lived in Iowa until the twins were eleven years old. During this time, Ellsworth had little chance to attend school because, as the oldest son, he was expected to spend his time helping the men who worked in the fields. When winter set in, however, and it was too wet to plow, Ellsworth did go to school—at least for a few months at a time—until he became too big to sit at the desks. At that point, he quit school entirely, after attaining what amounts to a fourth-grade education, and went to work full time for his father and uncles.

From then until he was twenty-four years old, Ellsworth stayed at home and helped support his family. But when his parents decided to go to Canada and homestead, he headed in another direction, choosing to try his luck in the Central Oregon town of Prineville. So, with a team of horses and the clothes on his back, Ellsworth Curtis departed for a life of his own.

CENTRAL OREGON

In 1907, Ellsworth and his brother Chester Curtis—along with Mother Emma Wilson, her son Bert, and two daughters, Abbie and Blanche, as well as Tom Coon—traveled from the Willamette Valley, over the Cascade Mountains, to Central Oregon. At this time, Lilly was in Prineville with her father. Although the Curtis and Wilson families knew each other, Lilly and Ellsworth didn't meet until later.

Tom Coon wrote, *The journey took us seven days to go across the mountains because we had wagons*

Ellsworth Thomas Curtis, 1909

and teams. We were all young and single and had lots of fun on the trip. Chester Curtis and Blanche rode in one wagon, Ellsworth and I in another, and Bert and his mother in the other one. Abby rode horseback and led another horse.

Chester had a twenty-two rifle with him, and he asked Tom if he would agree to fetch anything that Chester could shoot and kill. Tom agreed, and before they got out of the valley, Chester shot a big rooster in a man's barn lot. Tom relates, *Over the fence we both went, around and over briers, and because Chester had recently broken his leg and was slower, I won the race and captured the rooster. I put him in the wagon with Chester and Blanche, and they picked and dressed him while traveling along the road. We had to keep this from Mother Wilson, so we told her it was a China pheasant.*

The group stayed at the hatchery on the McKenzie River for two nights. They cooked their chicken and had it for dinner the next day. That morning, Mother Wilson asked the boys to dig a hole in the ground, about eighteen inches long, twelve inches wide, and eighteen inches deep for an oven. They did, and then the boys put a big bunch of live coals around the hole for her. Mother Wilson slipped a Dutch oven with a loaf of bread onto the coals and covered it with something that wouldn't burn.

Tom continues the tale: *We young bucks were full of vinegar and out for a good time. My sparring partner walked up and looked me over and then tackled me for a "rassle," and we went at it. In our scuffle, we stepped on top of the Dutch oven and trampled the whole top in, dirt and all. The bread was ruined. Mother Wilson just had a fit about it, and of course we young simps were dying laughing because we thought it was funny. We had to eat cold bread for dinner, but by that time everyone was in a good humor and the trouble was over.*

The next morning, on the third day, we went happily on our way. We got as far as Lost Creek and stayed there overnight. The water there was the coldest and the best tasting I ever had in my life. I just drank and drank, it was so good. My partner [Chester] said,

"I don't see how you can drink that." My answer was, "Why not?" He said, "This is from the Three Sisters" [a name given to three mountains located next to each other in the Cascade Mountain range]. *"As this was my first trip over this route, I didn't catch onto what he meant. My partner laughed till the tears rolled down his face, but so far I hadn't seen anything funny. He pointed and said, "There they are, the three snowcapped sisters." I guess if a person ever looked foolish it was me.*

After breakfast the next morning, we headed up the mountain for Alder Springs, where we stayed all night. We had pretty heavy loads in our wagons, so we doubled the teams on the heaviest ones. That left Mother Wilson, the two girls, and Chester and me, but we had a little bad luck. Abby, one of the girl bronc busters, saddled her horses and put the reins on the saddle horn, and then went to the spring to comb her hair. The horses took off down the mountain towards the valley. Blanche, Chester, and Abby went after them on foot, while Mother Wilson and I patiently waited. In the meantime, when the horses got to Lost Creek where we camped, the man who lived there ran out and caught them. They got on the horses and came back up the mountain in high gear, with Chester on one and the two girls on the other. They sure had the sweat flowing, when they got back to the spring. By then, the biggest part of the day was gone, and we still had to go seven miles up the mountain to Pole Bridge.

They made Pole Bridge by dusk and spent the night there. Tom tells how they spent some of their time: *Now, if you look on a big rock, in the opening at the spring, you will find all of our initials cut with a cold chisel and a hammer. If you look beyond that, you will find the marking of an old corral, where the people used to stop and corral their horses on their way to the valley, as these horses were wild.*

The next day, Tom relates, *We went to Cold Springs, where we stayed all night. The next day we went as far as Sisters, a small town at the base of the east side of the Cascade Mountains. The next morning we went on to Prineville, which was thirty-two-and-a-half miles. From Prineville we headed for the Wilson's homestead, out by Bear Creek Buttes.*

WILSON HOMESTEADS 1905

(Photo Credits: Lilly Wilson Curtis)

Bert Wilson's homestead house

Alwilda Wilson's homestead house

Lilly Wilson's homestead house

Lewis Wilson's homestead house

LANDSCAPES OF BEAR CREEK

(Photo Credits: Lilly Wilson Curtis)

Abby's good crop of potatoes

Woman on the Sand

Juniper and Pine trees

Clearing the brush to prepare for farming

Many people had gathered in Prineville to claim the free 160-acre land donations. They could keep the land if they built homes on them, thus, the name "homesteads." These homesteads were dry, with no water. The water had to be hauled in barrels with wagon and team, for both the house and the stock use. Gunny sacks were placed over the barrels to keep the water clean. The homesteaders were promised water within three years. That didn't happen.

Also, the homesteads were fenced with juniper posts and barb wire. One night, the Wilsons heard squealing and a lot of racket, so they went out to see what the racket was. They found a bunch of horses had run into the barb-wire fence. Some were tangled up in the fence, and the others were just simply cut up. As Tom Coon said, *It sure was a pitiful sight.*

There was a lot of horse stealing all over the range at the time, and they were suspicious that there was someone after the horses. About ten o'clock every night, the homesteaders would hear a band of horses go by some distance from the house. The horses were headed for the same spring they had hauled water from for themselves. About an hour later, they would hear the horses galloping back as hard as they could run.

There were a lot of coyotes on the desert. Blanche told Tom and Chester she had seen coyotes coming up to eat on dead calf every day—a calf the boys dragged up to about a quarter of a mile from the house. Tom writes, *We seen our chance to have some fun, for Blanche was very chicken-hearted. We told her to take her 22-rifle and go down and climb a juniper tree where the calf was, and she would have a chance to shoot Mr. Coyote. She did this and came to the house as proud as could be for killing the coyote. So we boys positioned ourselves to where she could hear what they were saying. We talked about what a cruel thing, to shoot a dumb animal when it is trying to get something to eat so it can live. Blanche broke down and cried, so our joke was serious after all.*

"That's the woman I'm going to marry," Ellsworth Curtis said to a friend, when he saw a petite strawberry-blonde crossing a street in downtown Prineville. That day, Miss Lilly Wilson wore a proper, ankle-length skirt, high-topped shoes, and a "waist," with long sleeves that covered her wrists. She wore a bustle over the backside of her skirt to hide her buttocks, and her waist/blouse had lace over her breasts so men couldn't make out her shape. Ellsworth began courting Lilly when they were both 25 years old. Lilly had come to Eastern Oregon for her health, as she was prone to asthma when she was living in the Valley. She had come from Halsey, with her brothers and father, because they had heard about the land give away.

According to her daughter Charity's memoir, Lilly went to Prineville in 1903 and worked as a schoolteacher in a one-room country school, District No. 6, Upper McKay Crook County. She also taught in Izee and Johnson Creek schools. She is listed in the book *Remembering School Days of Old Cook County*, by Irene Helms. Some of Lilly's students were as old as she was. Education in those years was sketchy at best, with some students only attending school in the winter months, when most of the boys wouldn't be needed in the fields.

After teaching for two years, Lilly went to Portland and was trained in the art of photography. She bought a large, wooden camera that stored its negative images on glass plates, and proceeded to take pictures of the people and places around her. Her photography studio was downtown, about a block from the Prineville Courthouse.

Of this time, Tom Coon writes, *Bert Wilson and Ellsworth Curtis stayed on the homestead, and the rest of us moved back to Prineville, where Allie Wilson, another sister was teaching school. Lilly had a photography gallery. Blanche started to teach school, and Chester Curtis and I got a job driving stage from Prineville to Rosland* [known today as LaPine]. *Abby got a job waiting tables in a hotel.*

ONE-ROOM SCHOOL, 1903

(Photo Credits: Lilly Wilson Curtis)

McKay School House

Lilly teaching

Students at rough-hewn desks

Students in Lilly's classroom

ONE-ROOM SCHOOL, 1903 (continued)

(Photo Credits: Lilly Wilson Curtis)

Two girls

Two students

Lilly and students at McKay School, 1905

Lilly Wilson, 1905 (Photo Credit: Lilly Wilson Curtis)

Lilly Wilson, 1905 (Photo Credit: Lilly Wilson Curtis)

PEOPLE OF THE TIME

(Photo Credits: Lilly Wilson Curtis)

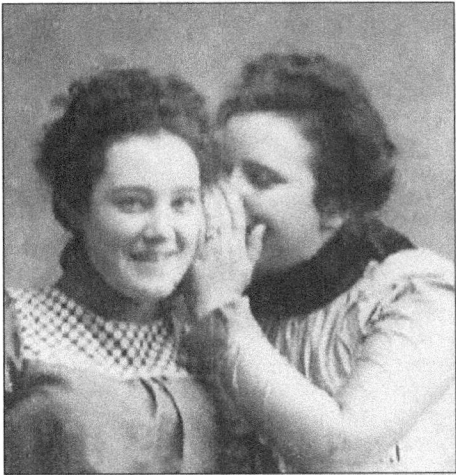

DANCES IN PRINEVILLE

In those days, one of the ways that young people got together was to go to dances. Tom Coon, who at one time was the police chief of Prineville, together with a person named Prince Glaze, sponsored dances. One such dance was promoted by the name of "Skook-Hum Hop." Tom writes that people would travel as far as eighty miles, by horseback or in rigs of any kind, to get to the Prineville dances. Sometimes all went well, and sometimes people brought alcohol, and things would get rowdy.

Tom Coon relates: *I went to a dance in Prineville one night, had a wonderful time— danced 'til midnight. I heard two fellows quarreling over a girl to see which one would take her home. She lived about five miles out of town, up Crooked River. One of these boys was standing with her at the top of the stairs, and the other ran and jumped on his back and rode him to the bottom of the stairs. By this time the crowd was coming down the stairs, and one of the boys was hollering, "Stay with me Tom, stay with me." I was about half way down the stairs, behind one of the musicians. I heard him say, "I'll separate them when I get down there." He had his big music rack folded up in his right hand. I was directly behind him ready to see that he didn't hit anyone with that rack.*

The fighters got separated, and I went in to the cloakroom to get my clothes. Some-

one had taken my hat, overcoat, overshoes, and umbrella. I had to stay all night in town. The next day, I borrowed an outfit from Ellsworth Curtis, then we went and had our picture taken [by Lilly]. I never did find my clothes, and I don't think either one of those boys got to go home with the girl. So, they had the fight for nothing.

Tom Coon and Ellsworth Curtis 1908 (Photo Credit: Lilly Wilson Curtis)

FREIGHT WAGONS

Ellsworth worked as both a ranch hand and a cowboy. He also drove a six-horse freight team carrying wool to Shaniko, which was the end of the rails in Eastern Oregon at that time. He drove freight between Prineville and Bend, as well.

Ellsworth Curtis and freight wagon (Photo Credit: Lilly Wilson Curtis)

According to Tom Coon, who also drove wagon freighters, *when the wagons were on the road there was no way to get around them until they stopped. There might be six or eight of these outfits halted at the same place to stay the night. Some of the freight wagons were loaded with liquor, and the freighters would often take a whiskey barrel, knock the hoop up, and punch a hole in the barrel with a nail so they could stick a straw into the hole of the barrel and drink "to their heart's content." When they were through, they would drive a wooden plug in the hole and very carefully drive the hoop down over the plug so no one would know. Soon, saloon keepers got wise and began weighing the barrels, making the freighters pay for every pound that was short.*

There was a rule of the road: If a freighter got stuck, any passing freighter had to pull the stuck one out. However, drivers would do everything but unload to keep from asking for help.

Sometimes, though, there was no alternative. Tom writes, *At times, in winter, between Prineville and Shaniko, when the ground would thaw out, the Shaniko flats were gumbo [mud]. The wheels of the freight wagons and stage coaches would fill up so full that you could not see the spokes, and they would have to take a shovel or a bar and dig the mud out. It was nearly impossible to keep going without doing this.*

MARRIAGE

Ellsworth and Lilly were married in Prineville on June 15, 1910, in Lilly's parent's home, with Reverend Lewellen officiating. As was the custom of the day, the couple was "chivareed" on their wedding night. This is a French folk tradition, in which the community gives a noisy, discordant, mock serenade to celebrate the couple's union. It

was practiced in much of the United States at the time, most frequently on the frontier. Each chivaree was unique and spontaneous. In some communities, the ritual served as a gentle spoof of the newlyweds, intended to disrupt—at least for a while—any sexual activities that might be under way. Friends kept the noise going until the couple gave up whatever they were doing and came out to serve their neighbors treats.

Tom Coon gives an account of his friends teasing him about getting married: *I really was*

Ellsworth and Lilly on their wedding day 1910 (Photo Credit: unknown)

bashful, but the people that knew me wouldn't believe it. I got an old-time friend, Ellsworth Curtis, to go up to the courthouse with me to get my marriage license. The County Clerk and his two assistants, Nora and Dora Sterns, knew me well. Ellsworth and I

Ellsworth and Lilly, 1910
(Photo Credit: Lilly Wilson Curtis)

walked up to the window of the Clerk's office, all braced and acting normal, and I told him I would like to get a pair of double trees that would not break. He said, "What do you mean Tom?" My answer was "A marriage license," and as they cost five dollars at that time, I had a five-dollar bill in my hand, and it got the darndest twisting of any five-dollar bill on earth. His answer was, "I guess I can't let you have it." Then they told me they were all out of marriage licenses. The two clerks were just dying laughing. After some talking, Ellsworth and I decided that someone had gotten my marriage license, and so we went out and sat on the courthouse steps and talked this over and planned what to do.

These two girls, whom I was raised with and went to Eastern Oregon with, Abby and Lilly Wilson, had a Photograph Gallery about a block from the courthouse. We had decided by this time that they were the ones who had my license. Ellsworth was courting one of these girls, so I was to go down there and sit on the steps, and Ellsworth was to go in. I was to have a sad look on my face. The younger one of the girls, Abby, came to the door and said, "Boone, what's your trouble?" My answer was, "I don't know what on earth I am going to do. I went to get my license and was told by the clerk that it was already gone!"

This girl was a great hand to laugh, and she had a loud voice, and every time she would catch her breath, she would holler "Oh, Lilly," which was her sister, inside. Lilly came to the door immediately to see what was the matter, so I explained my trouble to her, and while this was going on, Ellsworth, who knew where her purse was, slipped a five-dollar bill out of it. Then he came to the door and gave me a nod, as I knew he had the money. Here is where I made my mistake. I offered five dollars for the license. Lilly suspicioned something, ran in and got her purse and checked her money, and, while she was doing this, Ellsworth slipped the money to me. Then she jumped him for being in her purse, and he didn't deny it. This was on the twenty-fourth of November, and we were to be married on the twenty-fifth, Thanksgiving. Our license was handed to us when we were on the floor getting married.

DIGGING WELLS

Another story Tom tells concerns an adventure after he and Ellsworth were married: *During fire season, my wife and I, Estes Short, and Ellsworth and Lilly Curtis went out on the high desert, camped at Aspen Station, and dug wells for the government. We hauled all of our water to use for camp and for our horses from Button Springs.*

One day, Bill Slavens and another buckaroo were riding in the vicinity of Aspen Station, where the group was camped. They looked up this hill and saw a white horse, so they went around the timber line, and when they came out where they had seen the white horse, they could hear a bell, and, when they got up close, they recognized my old saddle horse. They said, "Here is where we eat a warm dinner.

Bill and his companion joined the campers for a meal. Apparently, Ellsworth and Lilly were there, too, because who else would have a 100-pound camera and a white horse on the desert.

As Tom tells it, *They begged us to take pictures of their outfit, but it didn't interest us at that time, because we thought it would be there forever. I would sure love to have some of those pictures to put in this* [his] *book.*

HONEYMOON ON THE DESSERT DIGGING WELLS

(Photo Credits: Lilly Wilson Curtis)

Button Springs; Dinner with Blue Mountains Camp Logging Company; Leaving Button Springs to go to Sands Springs; View from the buckboard; Dynamiting a well; Finished well at Button Springs; Finished Well

BUILDING A BRIDGE AT BUTTON SPRINGS

(Photo Credits: Lilly Wilson Curtis)

*Work Crew Tom Coon
and Ellsworth Curtis,
notice women to the right*

*Notice Ellsworth is
wearing Levi jeans*

*Men and women
working on bridge*

BRANDING CATTLE

Tom Coon remembers branding this way: *First the calves were to be weaned. We had five acres in the feedlot right by our house; we put our calves in where there was a fence between the mothers and the calves. The calves and the cows cried for two days and two nights. The calves were without feed during this time, then we fed them a load of hay, and they stopped bawling.*

Then it was branding time. We roped, branded, and marked 303 calves in one day. There were four of us on horseback. My wife and Mrs. Wilson kept the fire up and kept the irons hot, which we had more than four of them, if I remember right. Our brand on the cattle was P. C. O. on the left rib; our horse brand was bar horse shoe on the right shoulder.

We roped in pairs. Fred Merrit was my partner, and George Crosswhite and Clyde Leach were partners. My brother Leston Coon and Ollie Olson did the bull dogging, and Bert Wilson did the marking and branding. We had a gallon bucket hanging on the fence post to put the calf fries [testicles] in. These were taken to the house, cleaned, and cooked, and they were really delicious.

Now, there was never a calf that came to the fire without a rope on his head and one on his heels. We never crowded our horses out of a slow walk. We just rode into the corral, and one of us would toss our rope on the head, and the other person would catch him by the hind legs. We called this heeling, and we would changes ends of the calf, every other time.

Now you may laugh at me, but I believe in doing these things by the [Farmer's] Almanac or [astrological] signs. When the sign was between the hock and the foot, then it was time to do these things. I have marked hundreds of stock, such as calves, hogs, lambs, etc., and have got my first one ever to lose[No calf died from infection.].

These calves were turned loose in a pasture for a period of time, and then the next thing was to vaccinate to protect them against blackleg. We would round them up and drive them to the corral put them through the chute, which would hold thirteen at one time. Our vaccine gun held thirteen shots. I would get straddle of the chute over these calves and shoot them in the left shoulder. Then at the end of this chute we had a dodge gate, which would swing one way for the steers and the other way for the heifers, and that put them into different pastures.

BRANDING CATTLE AT BERT WILSON'S PLACE

(Photo Credits: Lilly Wilson Curtis)

Bert Wilson and Ellsworth Curtis;
Bert, Tom Coon, Ellsworth;
Ellsworth and Bert;
Ellsworth and Bert;
Job done

CROP HARVEST

We prepared for harvest by sharpening our sickles, oiled our mowers and started to cut the first crop. If we had plenty of water to irrigate with, we would get two crops a year, and this all depended upon the amount of snow, writes Tom Coon.

We cut our first crop, got it raked and shocked, and then came a thunder storm and soaked the shocks all the way through. In a few days, we would turn these shocks over, and before they dried out another storm came and soaked them again. We got the hay off the field and in the stack out of the way so the second crop could grow. Then after we got the second crop all in a stack, we would round up our cattle.

HARVESTING WHEAT

(Photo Credits: Lilly Wilson Curtis)

Harvesting wheat with a steam engine

Harvest crew (L to R) Emma, Ermine, Blanche, and Lilly, Clarence, Bert in
back row with flat straw hat others unidentified.

WOMEN'S CLOTHING STYLES CHANGE

French fashion icon Gabrielle "Coco" Chanel, born August 19, 1883, was the only woman to appear on Time Magazine's list of 100 most influential people of the 20th century. Along with Paul Poiret, Chanel was credited with liberating women from the constraints of the "corseted silhouette," by popularizing menswear for women and a sportive, casual chic as the new feminine standard.

With an influence extending beyond couture clothing, Chanel's ascendancy was the official deathblow to the corset, frills, fuss, and constraints endured by earlier generations of women. Under her influence, gone were the "aigrettes, long hair, and hobble skirts." Chanel's own look was as different and new as her creations. Instead of the typical, pale-skinned, long-haired, full-bodied women of the era, Chanel displayed a boyish figure, short cropped hair, and tanned skin—a distinct type of beauty the world came to embrace.

As early as 1915, the trendy magazine *Harper's Bazaar* raved over Chanel's designs: *"The woman who hasn't at least one Chanel is hopelessly out of fashion.... This season the name "Chanel" is on the lips of every buyer."*

By the 1920s, Lilly Wilson Curtis, who was only a year older than Coco Chanel,

Lilly in pants (Photo Credit: Unknown)

had embraced the new styles that allowed women such freedom of movement. She favored wearing pants and would eventually tell her granddaughters about the changes in fashion, noting that the first pants were pantaloons that gathered at the ankle. As an avid gardener and sportswoman, she wore jeans into old age.

Charity Curtis Bowers Memoir

Some of the following story was appropriated from a handwritten memoir by Charity Curtis Bowers, while other information comes from Charity Curtis Bowers' personal interview with the author. The written material has been edited for clarity.

In those years, Charity writes in her memoir, *that downtown Prineville, in the early twentieth century, every other door in Prineville was a saloon. Many a cowboy and sheepherder spent his wages, and sometimes his life, in one evening in these saloons. Someone would buy them enough drinks, and they would pass out. They would then be thrown out behind the saloon, minus all their hard earned wages. Sometimes they didn't survive the cold or the knot on their head.*

Charity also tells the story of her parents, Ellsworth Curtis and Lilly Wilson Curtis, and what she, herself, remembers from her remarkable experience as the child of early settlers to the Oregon Territories. *After a courtship of about three years, Mom and Dad were married. They moved from Prineville to a homestead 30 miles southeast of town, on Bear Creek.*

It was here, according to Charity, that Ellsworth and Lilly started the process of "proving up" on 160 acres of bare, sage-brush land. There were promises of irrigation water in the near future. As Charity remembers it, *Both, full of youthful vinegar, worked hard to clear the land, build a house, a barn, and a number of sheds for feed and implements. A cement cistern was placed under the house to which Dad hauled water from a spring. A hand pump on the inside of the house provided a means to bring water to the kitchen.*

On Mom's place, they built fences and hauled tons of rocks to the fence rows. These can still be seen on the bare land. Some of the rocks are so big that you wonder how Mom did it. They planted oats, barley, wheat, and potatoes. They depended upon snow and rain for moisture. Sometimes they lucked out, but more times than not, either there was no moisture, or it came in the form of hail and ruined the crops about harvest time.

THE HOMESTEAD YEARS 1910 TO 1918

(All Photo Credits: Lilly Wilson Curtis)

Ellsworth and Lilly on the porch of their homestead home.
The window was taken from Lilly's photography studio in Prineville.

Out building on the homestead

Out building

Lilly and Ellsworth inside homestead house

Ellsworth at future homestead site

Lewis Wilson with horses

Buck board and horses at neighbors

Ellsworth in Pine trees

Ellsworth with horse team

Ellsworth and friend out for a ride

Retrieving water for the home

top and bottom: Ellsworth with team and buck board

FARMING ON THE HOMESTEAD:

ELLSWORTH PLOWING WITH HORSES

FARMING ON THE HOMESTEAD:

ELLSWORTH PLOWING WITH HORSES (continued)

Ellsworth harvesting wheat

Piles of hay after harvest

Lewis Wilson behind horses

Abby's successful crop of potatoes

Ellsworth and Lilly had a few months to spend together on their homestead and riding around the countryside digging wells for the government, and then life took on a different phase. In those years, when you married, it was taken for granted that you start a family. At its best, the forms of birth control in those years were poor. The time of starting a family usually came soon after marriage.

A son was stillborn in 1911, and in 1913 another son, Lewis was born in Prineville. A daughter, Charity, was born on the homestead in 1915. Charity talks about her own birth and very early life: *Dr. Hyde came from Prineville and spent the night waiting until dawn when I was born. After I was born, he drove 30 miles back to town leaving the parents with the responsibility of a new baby. There were no hospitals in those days.*

Dad hauled wood to Prineville in the winter for a little extra money. One trip, he didn't return on the second day. Mom waited at the homestead with Lewis, a three-year-old, and, I, a baby. After the third day, one of the neighbors came to tell Mom that Dad had a bad accident on the hill going into Prineville. The brake on the wagon didn't hold, and the horses broke loose. Dad was thrown to the ground from his seat, and the wagon ran over his leg, crushing it. In a few days, he was brought home for Mom to care for. In time, he was back on his feet but walked with a limp for the rest of his life.

The summer I was one year old, there was an epidemic of rabies among coyotes. When the folks put the crop in that spring, Lewis rode with Dad, while he harrowed the ground. I rode with Mom on the seeder because they were afraid of leaving us under the trees, where we usually played. They were concerned that a wondering coyote could bite us. That summer, my grandmother Wilson killed a rabid coyote that wandered into her garden and couldn't find its way out. Can't you just see a little lady weighing less than 90 pounds beating a coyote to death with an axe?

CHILDREN ON THE HOMESTEAD

(Photo Credits: Lilly Wilson Curtis)

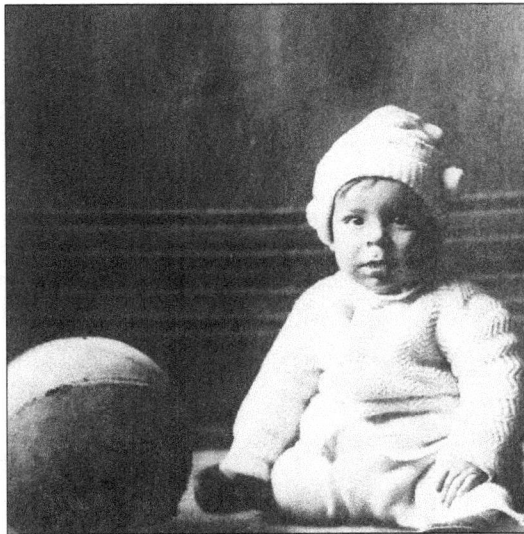

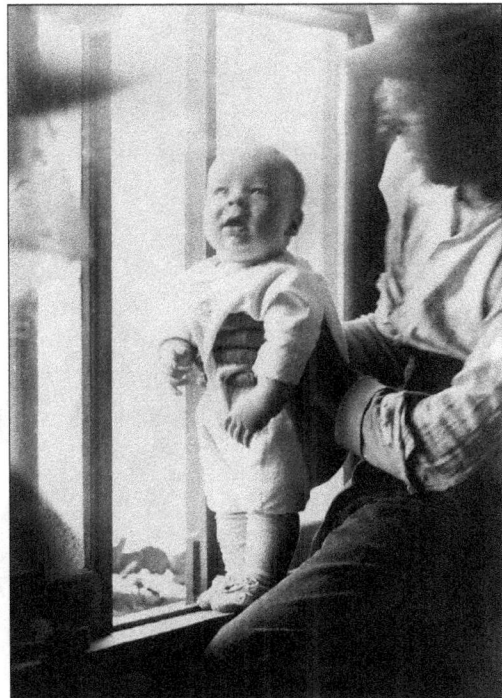

Baby Lewis Curtis above (R) Lewis with Clarence Wilson, 1913

Lewis with puppies

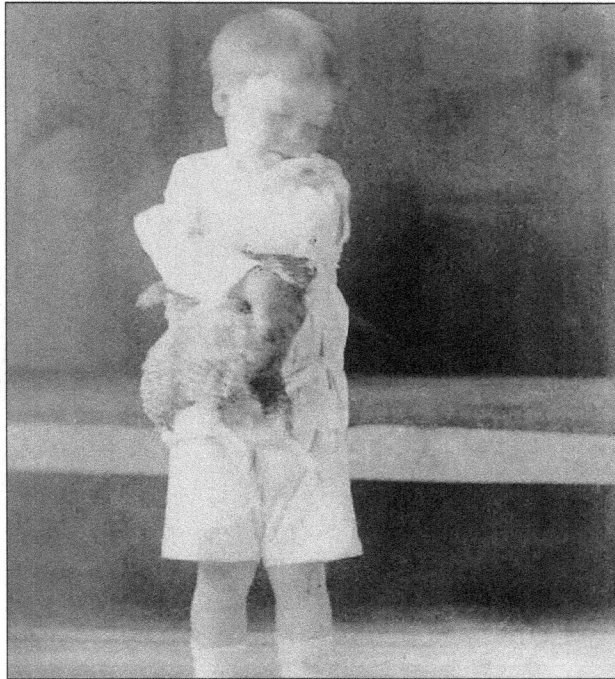

Lewis with chicken (top) Lewis in new clothes, 1914

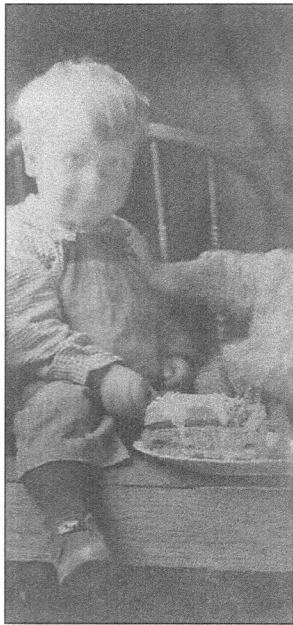
Lewis' birthday

Lewis with grifts: horse team from Grandpa Wilson and red cap and sweater from Grandma Wilson

Lilly, baby Lewis and Ellsworth

Lewis and Lilly

Lewis learning to eat

The Wilson's and Curtis' new cars. Ellsworth, Lilly and baby Lewis on the right, 1913.
This photograph was for advertising Clarence Wilson's car dealership on 4th St. in Prineville.

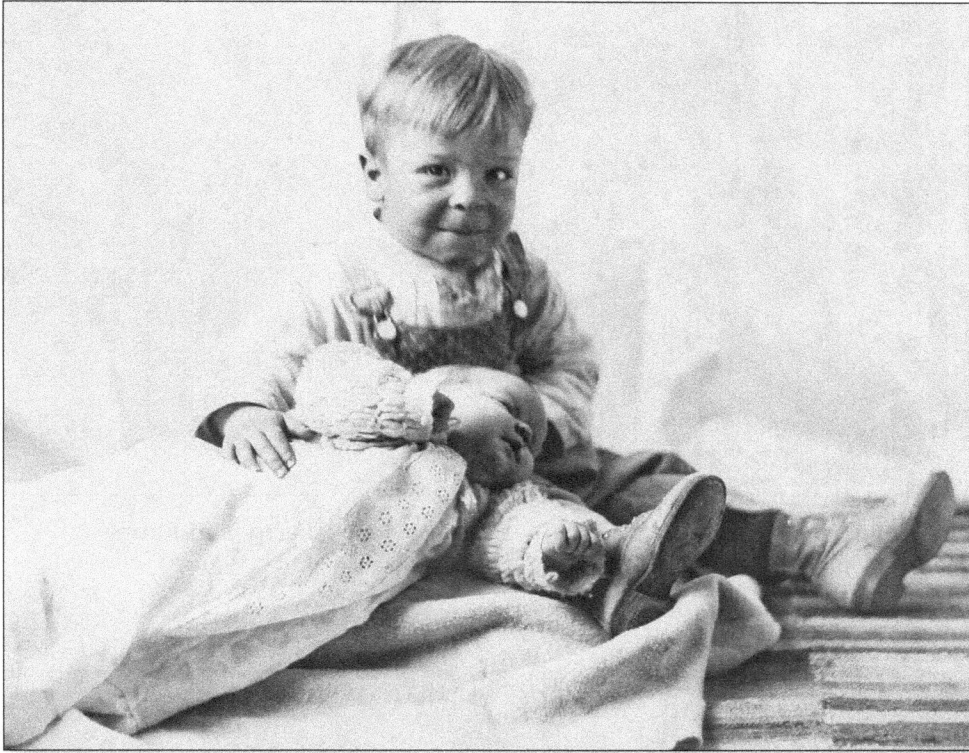

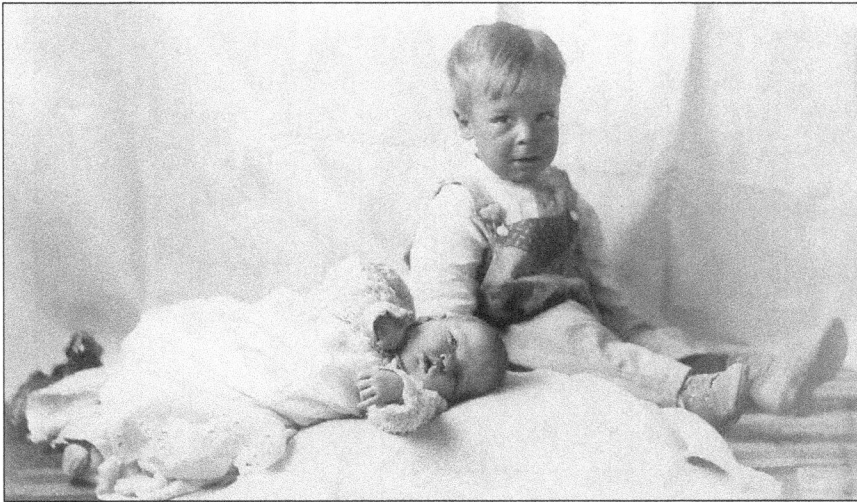

Lewis and baby Charity Curtis, 1915

Lewis and Charity with Grandmother Emma Wilson

Charity and Lewis

Charity and Lewis struggling with cat

Charity and Lewis

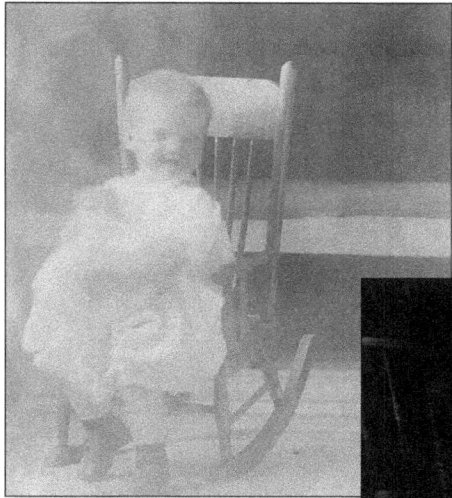

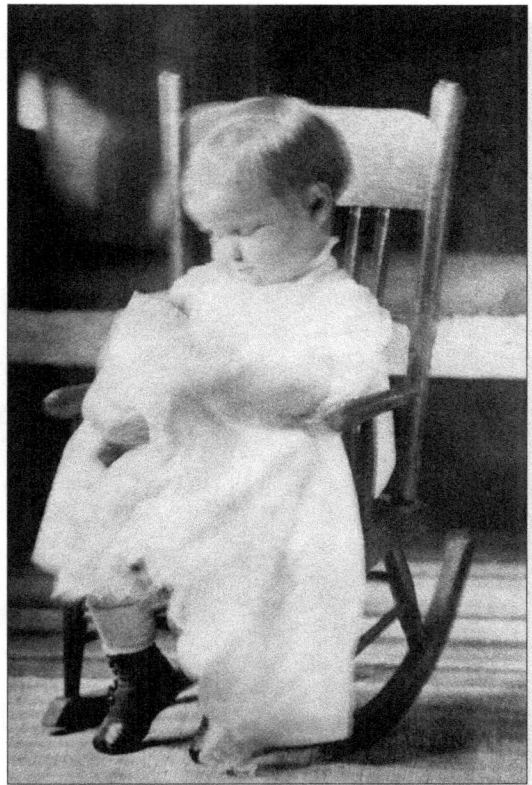

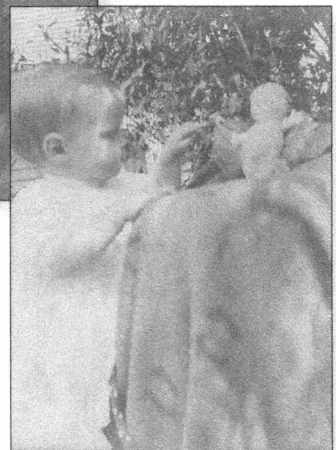

Charity Curtis on the Homestead

The folks survived on the homestead, suffering many hardships. One hardship was when Dad had a stroke that paralyzed his right side. He was only 34 years old at the time. The doctor prescribed using electric shocks, which came from a car battery he rigged-up for my mother to use. Miracles do happen because he got over the paralysis.

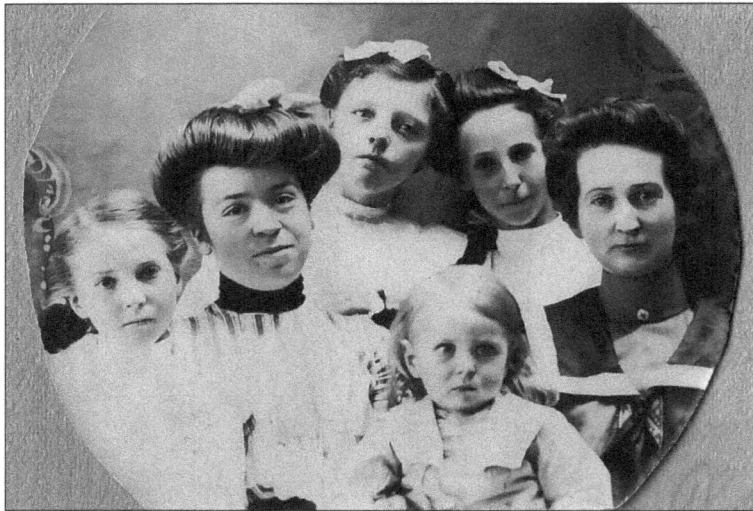

Lilly with Gladys Doaks and the Doaks children

Lilly and Ellsworth spent nine years on their desert homestead, where they struggled against cold weather, hail, heat and no water for crops. Sometimes they were lucky and had a good crop, but more often the hail would strike it down just before harvest. Charity recalls just such an incident:

After a hail storm wiped out a beautiful grain crop on July 4, 1918, the folks, hard as it was, decided they weren't going to make it. Dad had borrowed money to buy the seed. That fall they moved what few possessions they had back to Prineville. They moved into Mrs. Gladys Doak's house, a friend with whom my mother had lived before she married.

Doaks home in Prineville

Charity, Morris and Lewis

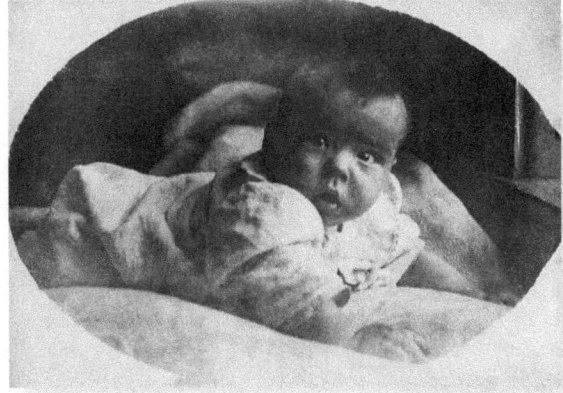
Morris Curtis, 1920

Ellsworth standing visiting with Tom Coon and friend
on a Sunday morning in town

Curtis family barnyard

Lewis, Morris and Charity, 1920

Morris Curtis, 1921

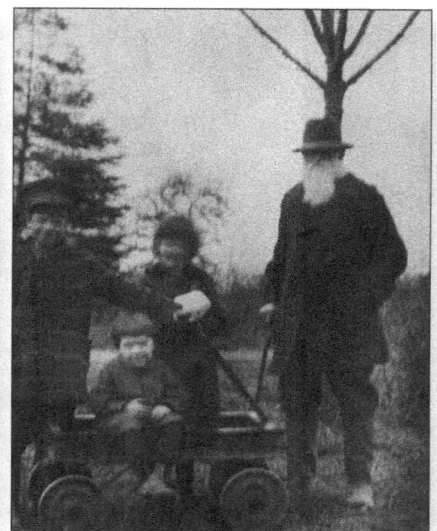

Lewis, Charity, Morris and Grandpa Wilson, 1921

In the spring, March 23, 1919, another son, Morris, was born in Prineville. And, Charity says, *Dad did odd jobs around town, or any place he could find work. The first Christmas I can remember was in Prineville. Dad built me a little cradle for my old doll. Mom made some new clothes for the doll, and Lewis got a little homemade wagon. Each of us received a stick horse. All the wood was painted a dark green. I remember this because the paint wasn't dry on Christmas morning, and we played with sticky toys all day. The following winter we moved, for a short time, into my Grandmother Wilson's house. I learned, in later years, she and my grandfather didn't live together as man and wife.*

My dad and his team of horses worked on the Ochoco Reservoir and on the Fresno, the winter of 1919 and 1920. He became very ill with pneumonia. Mom doctored him with old-fashioned homemade remedies, such as boiled onion poultices that Dr. Hyde told her about. Dad survived, and in the spring we moved to a small ranch about a mile-and-a-half east of town, where Dad again attempted to farm, and he also worked for the neighbor.

In that spring, Morris, then a year old, contracted pneumonia, and the folks sat by his bed, doctoring him in the same manner, with onion poultices for nine days, before the fever broke and he was out of danger. For years, as we grew up, my mother was partial to Morris, as she would always tell us how he nearly died and wasn't as strong as the rest of us. Whether this was true or not, it was always a thorn in Lewis's and my side, as we were punished and he wasn't.

During this summer, a baby girl was stillborn in August. I remember running through the field to tell my dad to come home. Mom needed him. I was barefoot, and the tumbleweed was plentiful, but I didn't stop until I found Dad at the neighbors'. He came home and took Mom to Mrs. Gladys Doak's home, where the baby was born.

This stillbirth was Lewis's and my first experience with death. We were shown the baby, and then we went home with Dad. We watched him build a tiny casket out of pine boards.

He and the neighbor buried the baby in the Prineville cemetery, alongside the brother who was stillborn before Lewis was born. In those days, women were kept in bed two weeks after a baby arrived, which may have been a good idea, given the way they had to work with no conveniences. Times were tough and not getting any better. (Years later, the folks erected a memorial stone for the babies in the Pine Grove Cemetery, near Halsey, the site of their own graves.)

That same summer, the neighbor's wife was injured in a horse and buggy accident, as she was delivering cream to the railroad station. The horse backed the buggy over the grade by the railroad station. She died a few days later, as I remember our family was the only people who went to the funeral. I will never forget looking down into the pine box and seeing the neighbor who took care of us while Mom recuperated from the birth.

We had more bad luck. Dad lost one of his young, year-old horses that Lewis had named Pepper. It fell into a cow stanchion, some way, and broke its back. After Dad put it up in a homemade sling, he eventually decided it wasn't going to get better, so he killed it.

That fall, Lewis and I started school in a little country school, east of town. We went about one month because the teacher spanked me every day, as I insisted on being left-handed. We then traveled to Hood River, where Dad picked apples, and Mom worked in

Bess and Tad Ellsworth's
last team

Bess and Tad

the packing shed, with Morris sitting in an apple box to keep him in one place.

Lewis and I again attended school. We soon found out that new kids aren't the most popular people. Everyone had their turn picking on us. They knocked us around and took our pencils. About the time we were finally accepted, the apple harvest was over, and we moved back to Prineville and into our Grandmother Wilson's house. We started school again, but by now we were used to being the new kids, and we didn't have so many problems. That year, we had a nice teacher and both finished the first grade that spring of 1922.

Sometime in the early spring, Lewis got the old push lawn mower out. He had it tipped

upside down and was running around the yard, seemingly having more fun than I was. I proceeded to grab the handle and take it from him, and as I raced by him with the blades spinning, he grabbed them. Disaster struck! He lost the first joint from his middle finger. It was just hanging by the skin. Seeing what I had done, I ran to the house and told Mom. She called Dr. Hyde, and

Flory, Ellsworth's horse

he said bring him and the finger in. The wash basin wasn't the cleanest in the world, but Dr. Hyde put lots of Lysol in some water and worked the blood off, centered the finger back in place, and bound it up. He told my mother to leave it like that for a week and smell it every day. This was done to make sure it was healing and not decaying. After a week, he unwrapped the finger and found that it was growing back. After that, Lewis always had a stiff-jointed middle finger, but it wasn't bad.

unknown horseman

In late May, the folks prepared to spend the coming summer up on Mill Creek. Dad had a job building fire trails with his team, Tad and Bess. He also had Flory, his favorite mare, which we kids rode.

Ellsworth with Flory

Mom had her fortieth birthday June first, and the night before we were to leave for the summer job, Prineville had a disastrous fire that burned most of the business district. As we had everything packed, we were sleeping in the basement of Grandma Wilson's house, when the noise woke Lewis and I up and we ran outside and saw the fires uptown. The folks both went to help with the fire. Dad was helping fight the fires, and I'm not sure what Mom was doing. They had the neighbor lady, Mrs. Campbell, come over to stay with us. We sat on the porch watching all the excitement.

This picture seems to show a chaotic scene near the Prineville Hotel. Was Lilly trying to get a picture of the fire?

Because we didn't have money to buy a license or gas, we left for the mountain with the horses and wagon. We spent all summer living in a tent. Our only source of meat was the fish that my mother and Lewis caught in Mill Creek. They were plentiful, but a diet of fish was monotonous.

One Sunday, after our Saturday night bath in the old tin tub, we were dressed in our clean clothes for the week. Lewis and I found an old salt trough and proceeded to push it into the creek and climbed in. In our newfound boat, everything went well as we drifted along, until one of us grabbed some willows, tipping the box out far enough to fill with water. It immediately sank, and neither of us could swim. But since we had ahold of the willows, we pulled ourselves out. When our mother got through with us, using the willows for another purpose, we gave up boating. So went the summer.

In the fall of 1922, Charity reports, the family packed a horse-drawn wagon and car and headed back to the Willamette Valley: *Fall came, and Dad and Mom loaded everything they could into a wagon. They even put a young calf in the back, hoping the cow would follow easily. Two horses were hitched to the wagon. One horse, Flory, was tied to the back. I rode with Dad in the wagon, and Lewis went with Mom in the 1915 Chevrolet touring car. Lewis held three-year-old Morris in his lap part of the time.*

The first thing that I remember is that we were met by an Indian and his wife. She had a child in a backpack. We had seen smoke in the mountains ahead. Dad asked the Indian if it was possible to drive through the fire area. But all the Indian would say was, "Ugh," and then he drove off. At this time, the McKenzie Pass was only wide enough for one-way traffic. If two vehicles met, one would have to back up to a place wide enough to pull off and let the other go by.

After the second day, the cow's feet became sore, and she wouldn't keep up, so Lewis and I took turns riding Flory and driving the cow. After we arrived on the west side of the mountains and came to the first farmstead where there was cattle, she went down the bank along the road and over to the barnyard fence. I wouldn't go after her, as I was too scared to ride down the bank, which I remember as steep. After much pleading from me, Dad got off the wagon and rode Flory down after the cow. That was the end of my riding the horse. Lewis rode the rest of the trip.

We camped along the McKenzie, somewhere up by Blue River. A lady that lived nearby brought a mess of fish nicely skinned—I can see those pink fish yet—over to our camp. The folks were pleased. I can't remember what we had been eating, probably sardines, bread and beans, and milk. After a diet of trout all summer, I could not eat more fish, so I imagine that I had bread and milk. It took us a week to cross the mountains.

We arrived at Grandpa Wilson's ranch at Nixon Station, where Mom's brother Bert lived with Grandpa. Mom's sister Alwilda (or Allie) spent the weekends. From the ranch, Allie rode the Oregon Electric to Albany, where she taught the third grade for over 30 years. The train had passenger cars that made several trips a day between Portland and Eugene. It was like a trolley car powered with electricity. At night, you could see the little spark glitter up where the line and rod from the top of the train connected, as the train raced by. It stopped at nearly every cross roads, some of which were McCarney and Nixon, to pick up eggs, cream, turkeys, chickens, and passengers. A few years later, I remember Dad sending eggs and cream. We raised turkeys and then killed and picked them by hand out in the cold barn. We left the head, feet, and each wing had three feathers left. The condition of the three feathers was the way the buyers could tell about the turkey's freshness. We bound them up and shipped them to Portland.

Once over the mountain, the family set about making a new life for themselves. Charity continues: We soon found a place to rent just west of Grandpa Wilson's ranch. Dad paid one-third of the crop as rent. Lewis and I started to school at Grasshopper School, two miles away. We walked down the country road in the mornings, and in the evenings we walked the railroad back. Sometimes, the neighbor, Mr. Leeper, gave us a ride. He drove an old, dilapidated truck, with smoke rolling up through the floorboards like you can't believe. Everything about the truck and Mr. Leeper smelled of oil and dirt. He would pick us up and haul us to school, where he was a janitor. No doubt he was one of the directors.

In those days, at the school, everyone drank from the same tin dipper. The water was in a bushel barrel that was pumped from the kitchen pump in the hall. Mr. Leeper swept the floor, sweeping the dirt down through the cracks in the floor, and built a fire in the old cast iron stove. Then he would go pick up the farmers' cream cans that were scattered around at different farms and haul them into Albany Creamery. In the summer there must have been some mighty sour cream because there was no inspection. The cleanliness of the milk was entirely up to each farmer.

IN 1923, BERT WILSON (PAT) WAS BORN TO THE GROWING FAMILY

(Photo Credit: Lilly Wilson Curtis)

Bert Wilson Curtis 1923

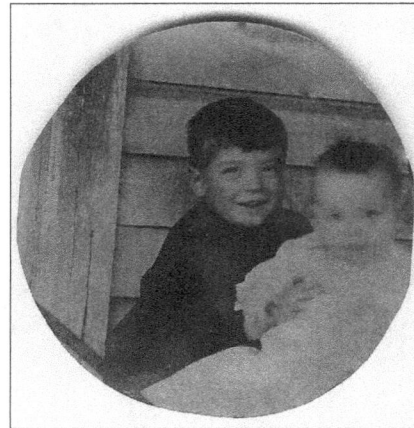

Morris and Pat, 1923

We lived at the house down from the Nixon Station ranch house, until Lewis and I were in the fourth grade. We moved a little southeast and lived on what was called the Burkhart Place. The house and other buildings were about a half-mile off the main road. We walked or rode Old Flory to school at Alford. We had a big snow in December, and the school was cancelled until January. When the first of the snow came, we turned down a ride with Mr. Starner, who came every day for his son and daughter. We all decided we wanted to walk in the snow. Mr. Starner told us "O.K., but I am not coming after you again." He kept his word, and we wished we hadn't decided to walk because the snow lasted two weeks.

Our next move was a few miles north, onto Nixon Road and the Mills place. We were back to our old school through the fifth, sixth, seventh, and eighth grades. Mrs. John Sayer was our teacher, and a very good one, until she left when we were in the eighth grade. Then we had Miss Florence Sisk. Since all of us had to take the state test twice, we didn't think the new teacher was much help.

In 1927 another baby joined the family: Martha Jean. That same year, our Grandpa Lewis Wilson moved in with us, and our family now numbered eight.

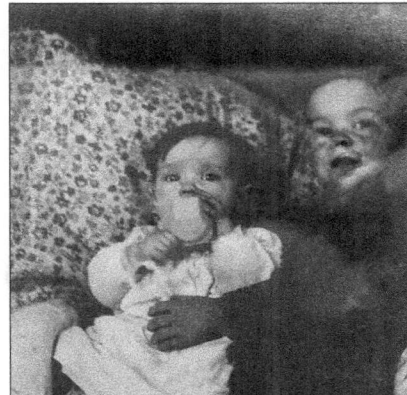

Martha and Pat, 1927

The fall of 1929 was the year of the Great Depression. We moved to Plainsview, a little wide place in the road. There was one store, one school, and one teacher, Mrs. Harrison, for the grade school, and Mrs. Allen, for the high school. She taught the English class for a year, and I didn't do very well. I ended up taking sophomore English my senior year at Lebanon. Lewis went one year and dropped out. I stayed out one year and then went back.

In 1932, we moved to the Jackson Place again, along Muddy Creek. I attended Harrisburg High from October until December. One of the directors sent my dad a letter requesting six dollars for my tuition, since we lived on the dividing line between Harrisburg and Halsey.

Pat and Morris attended school at Alford. We didn't have the six dollars, so Dad told me that if I wanted to go to high school, I could go to Lebanon and live with his folks. This would also help Grandma Curtis, who had heart problems. I became her housekeeper and cook. I did the washing and ironing. The next year my cousin Ethel wanted to go to Lebanon high, so she stayed with our grandparents.

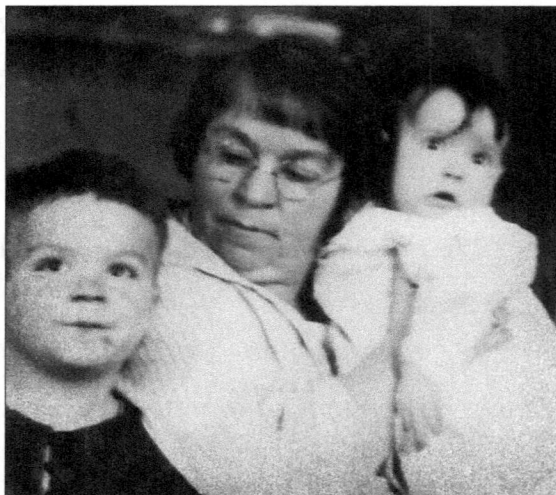

Pat, Lilly and Martha, 1927
(Photo Credits: Lilly Wilson Curtis)

Charity went on to have a long and healthy life. She received her high school education, trained as a hairdresser, and married Roy Bowers. Together they successfully farmed many acres in the Willamette Valley and raised four boys.

LIFE AT NIXON STATION RANCH

(Photo Credits: Lilly Wilson Curtis)

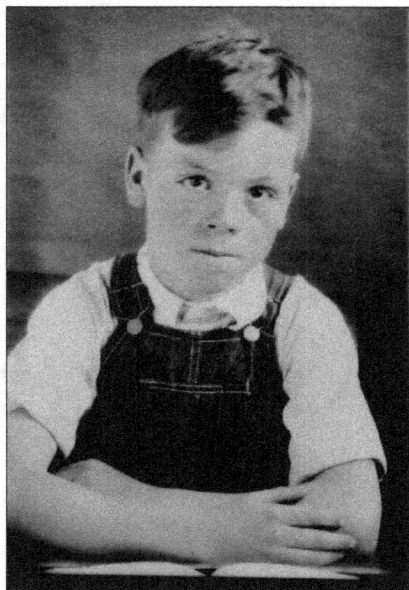

Bert (Pat) Curtis, 1927

Morris, Charity, Pat (on horse)
Lewis and Ellsworth

Lewis as a teenager

Charity Curtis

Charity Curtis 1930

Back row: Charity and Lewis, Front: Martha, Pat, and Morris, 1930

Group picture with cousins Lewis in the back left, Morris left in third row, wearing a hat, Pat in front of Morris in the bottom row and Martha beside him

Martha and Morris Curtis

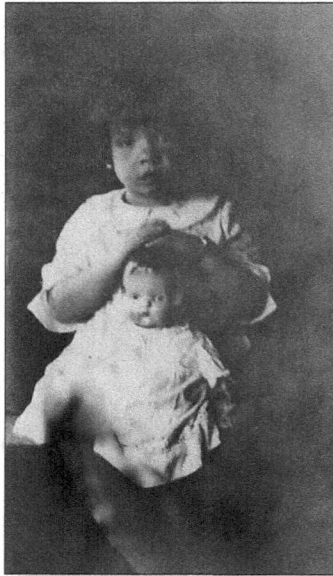

Martha and Pat Curtis

Martha and Pat Curtis, 1935

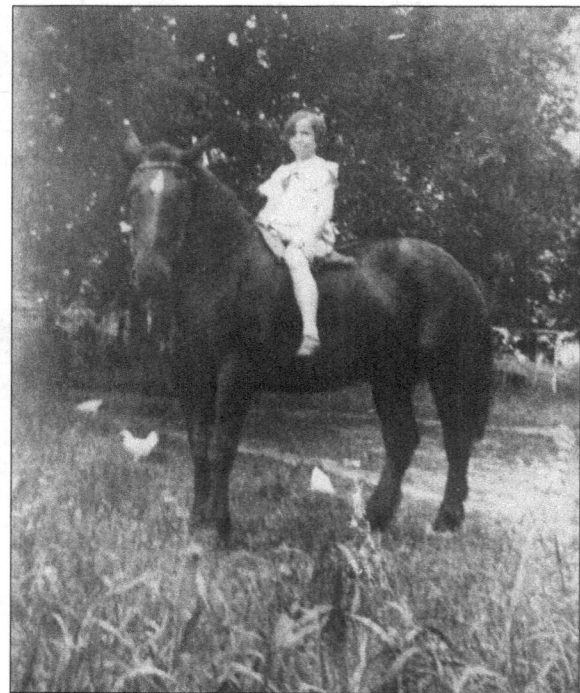

Martha Curtis on a horse, 1937

Grandpa Lewis Wilson on new John Deere tractor

Ellsworth and Lilly

Ellsworth Curtis near the
Nixon Station Ranch barn

Ellsworth and team

unknown horseman

ENDING A LIFE WELL LIVED

Meanwhile, Charity's parents, Ellsworth and Lilly, remained on the ranch at Nixon Station, farming and raising livestock. Grandchildren began coming into their lives, there were many challenges but all in all, Ellsworth and Lilly enjoyed numerous family gatherings and life was happy and abundant for a time. Their story began changing in the early 50s, when Ellsworth became ill with cancer. He had smoked roll-your-own cigarettes and a tobacco pipe his entire adult life, but, in those years, this habit was never a health concern.

When asked about her parents' relationship, Charity replied, "They probably had a few words now and again," but she felt they mostly got along and worked well together. She said of her father "He wouldn't cross anyone. If someone wanted something done, he did it."

Grandma Curtis with Paul Bowers one of the first grandchildren (Photo Credit: unknown)

Ellsworth and Lilly had a long and event-filled life. And if it is any indication of closeness, they slept in the same bed, until Ellsworth became ill in his 70s. For the three years of his illness, Lilly slept in a day cot just outside the bedroom. After Ellsworth died, Lilly moved to a small house in Halsey and lived another twenty-plus years. In her 90s, Lilly told a granddaughter that she thought of Ellsworth all the time and hoped to reunite with him someday.

Ellsworth and Lilly Curtis in their orchard, mid 1940s (Photo Credit: unknown)

A BRIEF HISTORY OF THE WILSON-CURTIS SIBLINGS

Firstborn son (stillborn, January 1912)

Lewis Wilson Curtis (January 21, 1913-1978) married Lavona Shanks in 1939. In 1947 Lewis farmed in the Valley but in the later 1940s purchased 185 acres in the Oregon-coast mountain range, near the town of Logsden. To pay for the property, Lewis and Lavona sold some of the land and felled a few of their trees, selling them to a mill. It was Lavona who ran the Caterpillar to load the logs onto a flat-bed truck for their transport, although, generally, Lavona was a homemaker, and Lewis farmed. He owned milk cows, worked as a logger, and for the Rock Creek fish hatchery, finally retiring from the Lincoln County Road Department.

Lavona had one son, Raymond, from a previous marriage. Lewis and Lavona had four children, together: Lois Alberta, who died at 18 months of pneumonia, then Lyle Duane, Nancy Sharon, and Margaret Caroline, all of whom, as adults, lived on the property near Logsden.

Lewis died in 1978, and Lavona died the following year. They are buried in IOOF Cemetery at Harrisburg.

Charity Curtis (May 16, 1915-2013) was trained and working as a beautician when she met Roy Bowers. They married in 1937. After their twin girls were stillborn, in 1938, Roy and Charity had four sons: Donald Ellsworth, Roy Dean, Paul Everett, and Robert Gayle.

The Bowers family lived outside of Harrisburg, Oregon, and made a living farming grass seed. Charity was the bookkeeper. The family formed Roy Bowers & Sons Corporation, in 1961. In 1972, Roy and Charity moved to Fort Rock and raised alfalfa hay on 430 acres. Roy passed away in 1987, and Charity died in 2013, at the age of 98. They are buried in IOOF Cemetery at Harrisburg.

Morris Merrick Curtis (March 23, 1918-unknown) married Audrey Hill. Two sons, Harold Morris and Darrel Leland, were born to this marriage.

Morris joined the U.S. Army and was stationed in the Philippines. When he returned, he trained as a pilot on the GI Bill, and then made a living crop dusting around Condon, Oregon.

After the war, Morris and Audrey divorced and he married Betty Ross, who had two daughters from a previous marriage, Betty Jo and Linda. Together, Morris and Betty had one son, George Allen. Later, they moved to Barrier, British Columbia, Canada, where they spent the rest of their lives. Morris lived into his 80s and was cremated upon his death.

Infant girl, Sara Jane (stillborn, August, 1920)

Bert "Pat" Wilson Curtis (May 7, 1923-1988) married Arlene Jackson, a U.S. mail carrier for 24 years. She gave him four children: Bert Wilson, Jr., Laurel Theresa, Marlene Ann, and Jay Ellsworth. Pat enlisted into the Navy during WWII. He had a rock crushing business in Brownsville and was a road supervisor for Linn County. He lived on a small farm outside of Brownsville until his death. He was cremated.

Martha Jean Curtis (June 30, 1927-2005) married Leslie Richard Gilbert (Rick) in 1946. She worked as a homemaker, waitress, and truck driver. Rick, who served in the U.S. Navy during WWII, was trained in a police academy in Stockton, California, and had a career in law enforcement. Martha and Rick had five children: Toni Patricia, Thomas Dale, Terrie Jane, Donna Sue, and Daniel Joseph. A sixth child, Amelia Louise, was born, to Martha, after the marriage ended.

Subsequently, Martha married Stillman (Tim) O. Daniels, in 1962. Tim worked as a log-truck driver and had seven children from a previous marriage. Martha and Tim combined their families and lived at the Nixon Station ranch for several years. After their divorce, Martha lived in Halsey until her death. She was cremated and her ashes were scattered near the ranch.

Sources

PRINT

Beckham, S. D. (1977). *The Indians of Western Oregon: This Land Was Theirs.* Arago Books: Coos Bay, OR.

Berg, L. (2007). *The First Oregonians.* Oregon Council for the Humanities: Portland, OR.

Coon T., Coon R. V. (1980). *A Coon's Tale.* Self-published.

Curtis-Bowers, C. (1983). A handwritten memoir of homestead years, plus an interview by Toni Gilbert, 2011.

Curtis-Kropf, V. (1983). *Family History and Genealogy of William and Georgiana Curtis.* Self-published.

Foner, N. & Fredrickson, G. (2005). *Not Just Black and White: Historical and Contemporary Perspectives on Immigration, Race, and Ethnicity in the United States,* Russell Sage Foundation: New York, NY.

Helms, I. (1980). *Remembering School Days of Old Cook County.* Prineville Print Shop: Prineville, OR.

Horn, J. (1994). *Leaving England: Adapting to a New World: English Society in the Seventeenth Century Chesapeake.* University of North Carolina Press: N.C.

Hoxie, F. & Nelson, J., editors (2007). *Lewis & Clark and the Indian Country: The Native American Perspective.* University of Illinois Press: Urbana and Chicago, IL.

Lazzerini, R. (2005). http://www.kindredtrails.com/Missouri-History-3.html. University of California: Santa Barbara, CA.

Moore, M. A. (1997). *Moore's Historical Guide to the Battle of Bentonville.* Da Capo Press: Boston, MA.

Schultz, J. (2000). *Encyclopedia of Minorities in American Politics: African Americans and Asian Americans.* The Oryx Press: Phoenix, AZ.

Shapiro, M. J. (1986). *Gateway to Liberty: The story of the Statue of Liberty and Ellis Island,* Vintage Books: New York, NY.

INTERNET

http://geography.about.com/od/historyofgeography/a/lewisclark.htm. Retrieved 1-9-15.

http://en.wikipedia.org/wiki/List_of_place_names_in_the_United_States_of_Native_American_origin#Oregon. Retrieved 1-7-15.

http://ows.edb.utexas.edu/site/hight-kreitman/land-bridge-theory. Retrieved 1-7-15.

https://sites.google.com/site/thenorthsite/early-immigration-in-the-u-s. Retrieved 1-7-15.

http://www.pdxhistory.com/html/railroads.html. Retrieved 1-14-15.

http://en.wikipedia.org/wiki/Coco_Chanel. Retrieved 8-30-13.

http://www.history.com/this-day-in-history/a-thousand-pioneers-head-west-on-the-oregon-trail. Retrieved 1-12-15.

http://en.wikipedia.org/wiki/Northern_Pacific_Railway. Retrieved 1-13-15.

http://arcweb.sos.state.or.us/pages/exhibits/1857/after/rail.htm. Retrieved 1-13-15.

http://en.wikipedia.org/wiki/Grand_Army_of_the_Republic. Retrieved 2-6-15.

http://en.wikipedia.org/wiki/Stagecoach. Retrieved 1-13-15.

http://www.infoplease.com/encyclopedia/us/oregon-state-united-states-history.html. Retrieved 1-13-15.

http://www.biography.com/people/sacagawea-9468731#early-life. Retrieved 1-13-15.

http://en.wikipedia.org/wiki/History_of_Oregon#Railroads_and_growth. Retrieved 1-14-15.

http://en.wikipedia.org/wiki/Paisley_Caves. Retrieved 1-14-15.

http://en.wikipedia.org/wiki/Fort_Rock_Cave. Retrieved 1-14-15.

http://en.wikipedia.org/wiki/Chivaree. Retrieved 6-1-14.

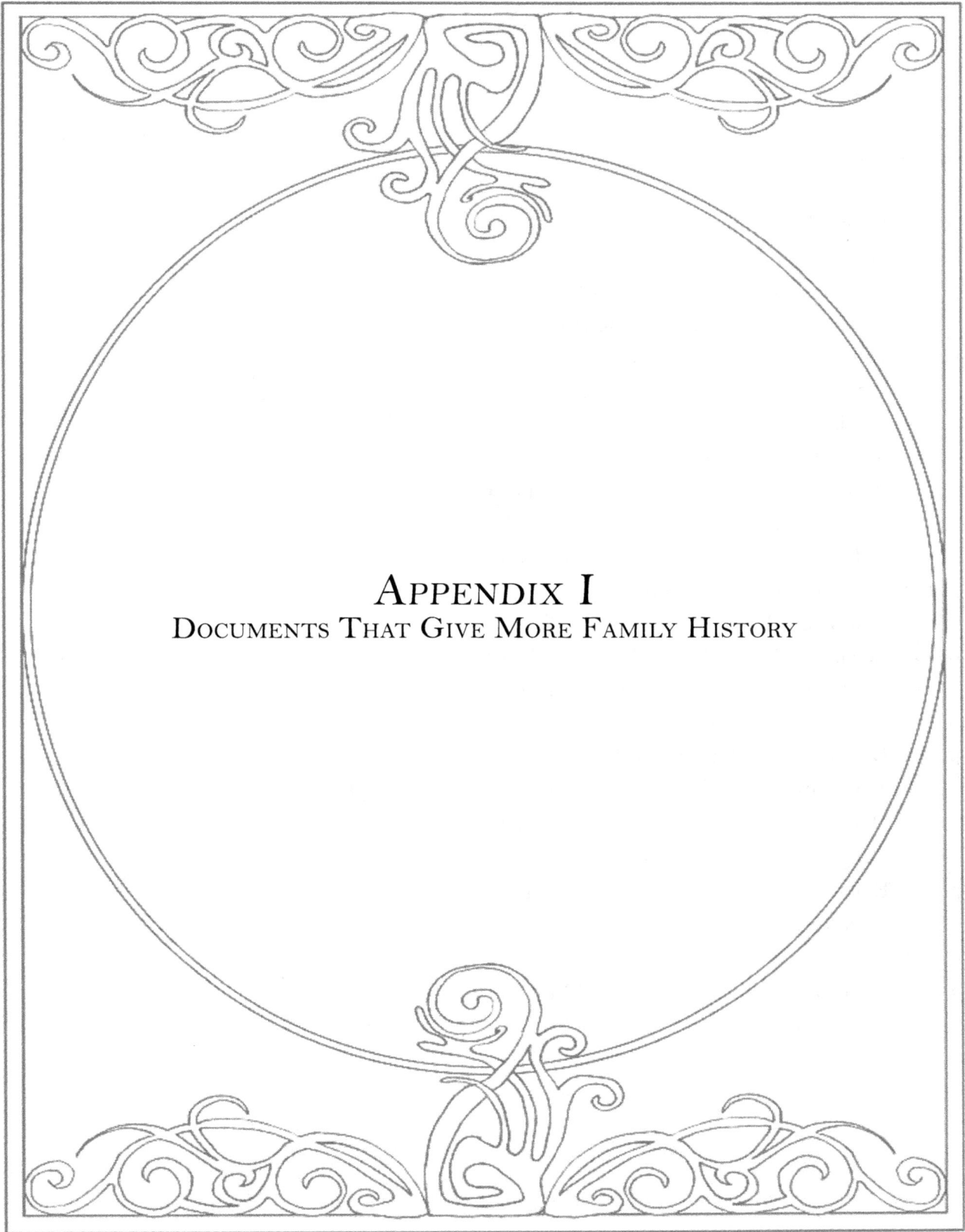

APPENDIX I
DOCUMENTS THAT GIVE MORE FAMILY HISTORY

Appendix I

pp. 167, 168: Lilly's teacher souvenir with pupils' names.

p. 169: Teacher's contract.

p. 170: Lilly's driver's license

p. 171: Homestead Application

p. 172: Lilly Wilson Curtis birth certificate

p. 173: Lewis Wilson's discharge papers from the US Army

p. 174: Lewis and Rufus Wilson in Oregonian Newspaper Sept. 27, 1905

p. 175: Lewis and Rufus Wilson Newspaper picture

p. 176: Lewis and Rufus Wilson Newspaper picture

p. 177: Multiple sets of twins to the family with history

p. 178: Rufus and Lewis Wilson civil war encampment

p. 179: Rufus and Lewis Wilson newspaper article

p. 180: Rufus and Lewis Wilson newspaper information

p. 181: Rufus and Lewis Wilson

p. 182: Lewis and Rufus Wilson

p. 183: Lewis and Rufus Wilson Civil War interview

p. 184: Civil War story and picture with Lilly on the right

p. 185: Two sets of twins

p. 186: Document of Homestead Property

p. 187: Newspaper account of Emma Wilson not contesting Lewis' will

p. 188: Doctor's order to transport Emma Wilson by ambulance from Prineville to Portland Oregon due to appendicitis 1931

p. 189: Eviction notice to Clarence Wilson from Lewis Wilson

p. 190: Alwilda Wilson obituary and history of Blanche Wilson's husband

p. 191: Emma Wilson interview

p. 192: Information about Thomas and Mary Ann Watson

p. 193: Lilly having fun

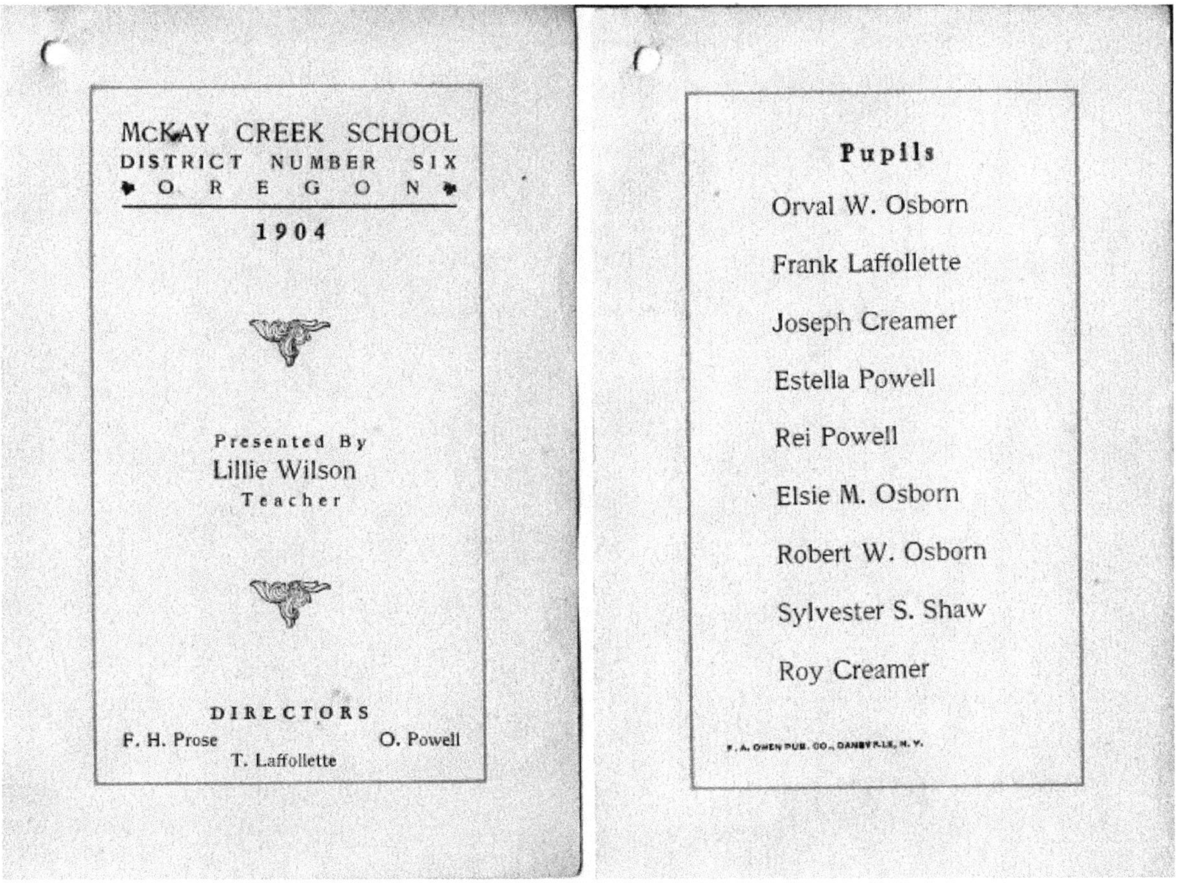

McKAY CREEK SCHOOL
DISTRICT NUMBER SIX
♦ O R E G O N ♦

1904

Presented By
Lillie Wilson
Teacher

DIRECTORS
F. H. Prose   O. Powell
T. Laffollette

Pupils

Orval W. Osborn

Frank Laffollette

Joseph Creamer

Estella Powell

Rei Powell

Elsie M. Osborn

Robert W. Osborn

Sylvester S. Shaw

Roy Creamer

F. A. OWEN PUB. CO., DANSVILLE, N. Y.

Teacher souvenir and pupils

Appendix 167

Teacher souvenir

[55]

TEACHER'S CONTRACT.

| DUPLICATE. |

This form is to be filled, detached on the perforated lines, and handed to the teacher. This Contract must be signed by at least two Directors of the School District.

It is hereby agreed between the Directors of School District No *3* of *Crook* County and State of Oregon, and *Miss Lilly Wilson* a legally qualified teacher of said County and State, that the said *Lilly Wilson* is to teach the public school of said district for the time of *Five Months* [Here insert the time.] for the sum of *Forty Five (45)* dollars per month, commencing on the *24* day of *Sept,* *1906,* and for such services, lawfully and properly rendered, the Directors of said district are to pay to the said *Lilly Wilson* the amount that may be due according to this contract, on or before the *8* day of *February* *1907*

Dated this _____ day of *September 1906*

Wm. H. Birdsong
S. E. Strand

Lilly Wilson Teacher.   Directors of School Dist. No. *3*, of *Crook* County, Or.

Teacher's contract

Appendix 169

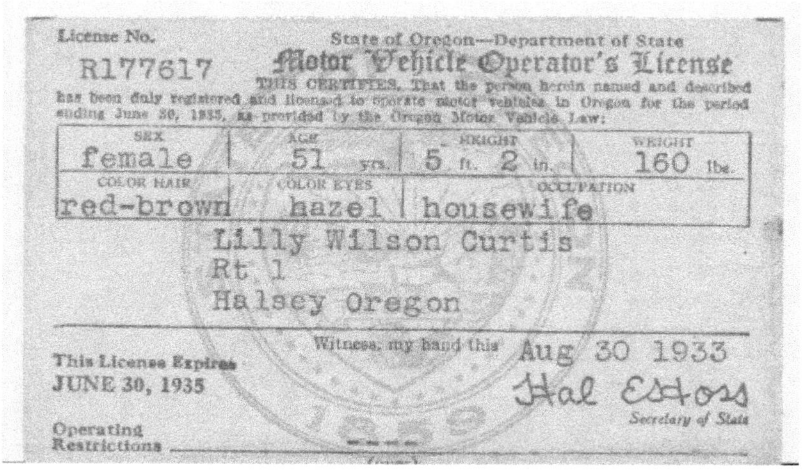

License No.

R177617

State of Oregon—Department of State

Motor Vehicle Operator's License

THIS CERTIFIES, That the person herein named and described has been duly registered and licensed to operate motor vehicles in Oregon for the period ending June 30, 1935, as provided by the Oregon Motor Vehicle Law:

SEX	AGE	HEIGHT	WEIGHT
female	51 yrs.	5 ft. 2 in.	160 lbs.
COLOR HAIR	COLOR EYES	OCCUPATION	
red-brown	hazel	housewife	

Lilly Wilson Curtis
Rt 1
Halsey Oregon

Witness, my hand this Aug 30 1933

This License Expires
JUNE 30, 1935

Hal E. Hoss
Secretary of State

Operating
Restrictions ----

Lilly's drivers license

DEPARTMENT OF THE INTERIOR.

UNITED STATES LAND OFFICE,

The Dalles, Oregon, March 8 ,1907.

Mr. Lewis R. Wilson,

Prineville, Oregon

Dear Sir:

I hereby acknowledge receipt of the papers in your .....
homestead application ...., for

SW¼ .... Section 4, , Township 18,S. ,

Range 16, E.W.M.: also the enclosure of $16.00 .

There being a temporary vacancy in the office of register, all
business requiring the action of both officers must await the fill-
ing of the vacancy.

Applications to contest entries, or to enter land, and all
other applications requiring joint action of officers will be filed
as presented but not acted on until business is resumed, when they
will be disposed of in their order.

The land office remains open for the hearing of final proofs
now advertised and for the information of the public.

Yours respectfully,

Receiver

Homestead application

TO THE CIRCUIT COURT OF THE STATE OF OREGON

For the County of Linn

IN THE MATTER OF THE
REGISTRATION OF THE BIRTH
of

................LILLY W. CURTIS................
Petitioner

No...924....

REGISTRATION OF BIRTH
DECREE FOR

The petitioner, ...Lilly W. Curtis.................., whose race or color is ....white...., being a resident of the State of ....Oregon.........., living at ......Route 1............ Street, City of ....Halsey.............. and having filed a petition for the registration of ..her.. birth, and having served a copy thereof upon the district attorney of this county, and more than five days having elapsed since the service and filing of said petition;

And the court having held a hearing upon said petition and being satisfied that the facts stated therein are supported by substantial evidence, hereby finds that petitioner was born at ....Waukee............., in the County of ....Dallas....., State of ......Iowa.........., on the ..1st.. day of .....June........, in the year ..1882;

The petitioner's father was ....Lewis Ramsey Wilson......, of the City of ...Waukee.., State of ...Iowa...... who was born at ......Industry......, ...Illinois.... on the ..24th. day of ...Oct..1841., and that petitioner's mother was .....Emma Wilson............, of the City of ....Waukee................., State of ....Iowa.............., whose maiden name was ..Emma Karrick...................... and who was born at .....Industry................., ..Illinois...., on the .2nd. day of ..... September......., 18?? That said petitioner's maiden name was Lilly Wilson.

IT IS, THEREFORE, hereby ordered that the birth of said petitioner be registered by the State Registrar of Vital Statistics.

Done in open court in duplicate this ..4th.. day of ...December......., 194.5.

(SEAL)

......L. G. LEWELLING............
Circuit Judge

STATE OF OREGON
County of Linn. } ss.

I, R. M. Russell, County Clerk of Linn County, Oregon, and Clerk of the Circuit Court of said County and State, do hereby certify that the foregoing copy of Decree for Registration of birth is a full, true and correct copy of the original Decree of Registration of Birth of ....LILLY W. CURTIS.................... as the same appears of record in my office.

In Testimony Whereof, I have hereunto set my hand and affixed the seal of the Circuit Court of Linn County, Oregon, this ....4th... day of ...December......., 194.5.

.....................................County Clerk

By .... Deputy

Lilly's Birth Certificate

Lewis Wilson's discharge papers from the US Army

Appendix 173

BROTHERS MEET AT EXPOSITION FOR FIRST TIME IN TWENTY-FIVE YEARS

CAUGHT WITH BAG OF OPIUM

Pullman Car Superintendent Says He Is Victim of Circumstances.

Lewis and Rufus Wilson in Oregonian Newspaper Sept 27, 1905

Lewis and Rufus Wilson newspaper picture

Lewis and Rufus newspaper article

at Wilson Family R...

Two Other Sets of Twins Also to Be at Gathering

When Bobby and Betty Applegate, 6, of 4514 Woodlawn Ave., attend the annual reunion of the Wilson family early in June at Macomb, Ill., they will be the youngest of four sets of twins surviving in the family.

The oldest pair of twins, Rufus and Lewis Wilson are 90 and veterans of the civil war. [illegible] lives in Halsey, Ore., and [illegible] Waukee, Iowa.

It happened this way:

About 100 years ago, John Wilson and Martha Vance were married. They had 12 children. Two of them, Rufus and Lewis, were twins.

Another brother James was married and had twin sons, Melvin and Calvin.

A sister was married and had twins. The sister's granddaughter who is Mrs. Emery Applegate, is the mother of the youngest set of twins, Bobby and Betty.

Harriet and Harold Epps, 8, also twins, are the grandchildren of one of the nonegenarians, Rufus and Wilson. None of their aunts or uncles are twins. Another set of twins, grandchildren of the former Wilsons, died.

Twins occur about once in a hundred births, according to the Encyclopaedia Britannica, which also says that the tendency to have twins is liable to be hereditary.

The Wilsons think so, anyway.

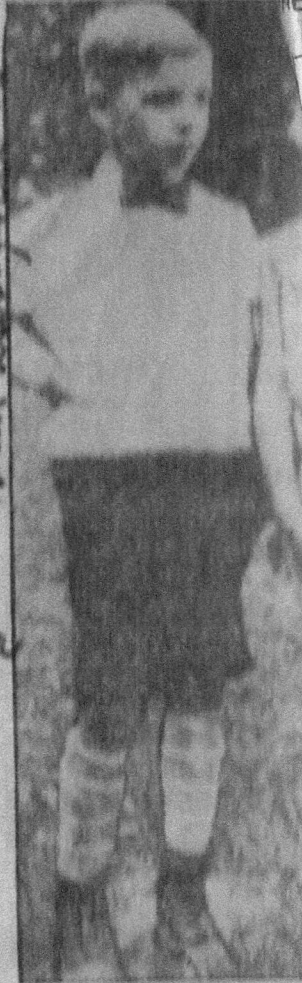

Bobby and Betty

Multiple sets of twins to the family...history of twins parents

THE OLDEST TWINS OF THE BLUE who attended the G. A. R. national encampment at Des Moines are Rufus R. Wilson, at the left, and Louis R. Wilson. The former now lives at Halsey, Ore., the latter at Waukee, Iowa. They are 85 years old.
(Photograph from Pacific and Atlantic)

Rufus and Lewis Wilson Civil War encampment

TWINS POSE—Rufus Wilson, Waukee, Ia., and his twin brother, Lewis Wilson of Halsey, Ore., got together recently and recalled the days of the civil war when they served together as members of Company I, 78th Illinois regiment. They are 90 years old. (Kobel.)

Rufus and Lewis Wilson

STRANGE AS IT SEEMS— By John Hix

A MONUMENT
TO THE DEVIL —
Erected by the Yezidis
of Eastern Asia . . .

THE OLDEST TWINS
IN THE UNITED STATES —
RUFUS AND LEWIS
WILSON,
aged 90,
BOTH FOUGHT
IN THE
CIVIL WAR . . .

THE SPONGE - an animal -
CAN BE CUT ALL TO PIECES
WITHOUT DYING . . .

WHAT'S IN A NAME?

MR KOW IS PRESIDENT
OF THE CHUNG WAH
MEAT CO.
of Honolulu, Hawaii

I. STEELE IS A
POLICEMAN
in Elkhart, Ind . . .
CONTRIBUTED BY
R. L. WILKINS
• • •
POPCORN IS THE
NAME OF A
POPCORN PEDDLER
near Jonesboro, Ga.
SENT IN BY
RUSSELL JAMES

© McClure Newspaper Syndicate

To the Yezidis (devil worshippers) the powers of evil are as mighty as the powers of good. Consequently, Satan has his day with these strange folk for they believe that although he is undergoing punishment for disobedience to the divine will, he is still chief of the angelic hosts. They also worship Christ and Allah or the Supreme Being and the Sun.

The monument shown in today's cartoon was erected at Adekh Aqi, in the valley lying between the Tigris and Euphrates rivers in Eastern Asia. Yezidis are found also in Africa, Asiatic Turkey, and Armenia and number more than 200,000.

Although sponges have all outward appearances of plants they are actually living organisms of the animal kingdom. Dr. P. G. Galtsoff, of the United States Bureau of Fisheries, has found that a sponge can be cut into numerous minute segments which will grow together again and become a living whole, the cells of a like order hunting their own several neighbors and a other

Rufus and Lewis Wilson were born in McDonough County, Illinois, October 26, 1841, the sons of the first couple married in that county. Rufus now lives in Waukee, Iowa and Lewis in Halsey, Oregon.

• • •

Any reader wanting further proof of anything depicted here should address the author, care of this paper, and enclose a stamped and self-addressed envelope for reply.
JOHN HIX.

Lewis and Rufus in newspaper

Appendix 180

OLDEST CIVIL WAR TWIN VETS

Lewis and Rufus

BROTHERS MEET AT EXPOSITION FOR FIRST TIME IN TWENTY-FIVE YEARS

LOUIS R. WILSON, OF HALSEY, OR., AND RUFUS R. WILSON, OF WAUKEE, IA.

Louis R. Wilson, of Halsey, Or., and his twin brother, Rufus R. Wilson, of Waukee, Ia., met for the first time in years in this city last week. The brothers were here visiting the Exposition, when they met at the home of a sister-law. They are veterans of the Civil War, having served through the strife between the North and South in the organization—Company I, of the Seventy-eighth Illinois Infantry.

Lewis and Rufus Wilson

TWINS AGED 90,
CIVIL WAR VETS,
TO BE IN ALBANY

TWIN CIVIL WAR VETERANS NEARLY 90 YEARS OLD

LEWIS (LEFT) AND RUFUS WILSON.

TWINS, ALBAN

Nonogenar
War E

PAIR 'KID

Wilson Broth
and Lew
Enjo

Lewis and Rufus Wilson Civil War history

Twins, 85, Attend G. A. R. Convention

WHICH is which?
That is what the boys in company L, Seventy-eighth Illinois infantry, thought when Rufus and Louis Wilson joined them way back in 1862.

Delegates to the G. A. R. encampment thought the same thing yesterday, when these 85-year-old "twin boys" arrived.

Rufus motored here from Halsey, Ore., and met Louis at Waukee, Ia.

They enlisted together in 1862 and told their companies that they hailed from "tthe devil's half acre," McDonough county, Ill.

"Before long the boys knew we were telling tthe truth, for we were two of the 'meanest' in the company," they said.

They have been in skirmishes by the score and at least a dozen battles.

Quincy, Ill., was their training camp under the direction of Capt. G. H. Runnells. From Quincy they marched to Louisville, then to Nashville and Franklin, Tenn.

They had no actual battles until the three-day fight at Chickamauga, Sept. 18, 19 and 20, 1863. After that it was Mission Ridge and Lookout mountain.

Then Sherman's famous march to the sea!

"We had one good meal on that march," they said. "Twelve of us went out and foraged a __ apiece. Then we made __ ate everything but two __ mush.

"We expected to wake __ find ourselves dead, aft __ stuffing."

a inheritance taxes, unnecessary. The time is coming whe __ of the entire state. will refuse to be exploited any longer than this, and levy day can be postponed for a long time ese profits for the ping their independence and their in hole.

Lewis and Rufus Wilson Civil War history

daughter, Mrs. C. T. Curtis. Last Friday Rufus came from his home at Waukee, near Des Moines, Ia., to visit his twin and comrade brother.

To the best of knowledge these two are now the only twins now living who were bona fide soldiers in either the Union or Confederate armies. Some years ago at a G. A. R. encampment the Wilsons met another pair of twins who had fought for the Union. Since then one of those two has died. Moreover, they were younger than the Wilsons and were from different states and in different regiments. The Wilson twins fought side-by-side for more than two years.

Pair Together in War.

Lacking two months of being 21 years old, Lewis and Rufus Wilson enlisted in company 1, 78th Illinois regiment, in August, 1862. Not until General Sherman and his army reached Atlanta, Ga., were they ever separated, and then they remained in the same regiment.

The Wilson twins were born at Industry, McDonough county, Illinois, October 26, 1841. Their parents, Mr. and Mrs. John Wilson, were the first couple married in that county. The brothers remained at home until the cause of freedom called them. They returned to Industry after the war, but a few years later Rufus moved to a farm at Waukee, Ia. Bonds of brotherhood and comradeship would not remain broken so Lewis soon followed his brother. He settled on a farm adjacent to that of his brother. Both grew corn there until Lewis heard another call. It was that of the west. In February, 1885, he came to Oregon with his wife and family and farmed near ▓▓▓▓ until two years ago, when he went to Plainview.

Visit Second to Oregon.

His present visit is Rufus' second with his Oregon twin brother. And Lewis also has gone back to Waukee several times. Last year he went to see Rufus. On two previous visits the two together attended G. A. R. conventions.

Exchange of banter is the chief diversion of these two brothers, whose lives have been more closely interwoven than those of most kin.

"Why did you finally separate?" Rufus was asked.

"They wouldn't let Lewis stay at Waukee," Rufus said, smilingly.

"I wanted more adventure but Rufus showed the white feather," Lewis retorted. And so they talk, pausing now and then to live over again their long and eventful lives.

Both Lewis and Rufus Wilson vote emphatically in favor of the motion that Sherman was right. "It sure was hell," Rufus said. Neither of the veterans relishes recollections of the dark side of the war. While they escaped harm themselves they parry questions about the shot and shell phase of their service. Even when exchanging reminiscences with each other alone they dwell upon their pranks and youthful escapades rather than upon their achievements at arms. No boasting passes their lips.

"I'll never forget the day I discovered I was a sprinter," Lewis said. He alluded to a time when his infantry regiment was attacked by rebel cavalrymen. "We had orders to retreat and I sure obeyed them," Lewis recounted. "We raced to a swamp, where they couldn't follow us, but it seemed to me I was standing still until I realized I had outstripped those horses. I guess I was about the fastest man in our regiment that day."

"Where were you all this time?" Rufus was asked.

"Right ahead of Lewis," Rufus replied.

Civil War newspaper story and picture of Lilly on the right

Just Two Sets of Twins

Here are the oldest and youngest pairs of twins entered in the annual "Twin Round-up" at Albany, Ore. The 90-year-old pair, Rufus, left, and Lewis Wilson, Civil War veterans, won as the oldest, while the three-months-old twins, Marjorie, left, and Kenneth Myer (held by Mrs. Gladine Senkey) won the youngest.

Two sets of twins

Land Patent Image

Acc./Ser. Nr.: 188758   Patentee: LEWIS R WILSON
Issue Date: 4/8/1911

Image Formats: Small GIF | Large GIF | TIFF | PDF

THE DALLES 04092.   4—1008-R.

The United States of America,

To all to whom these presents shall come, Greeting:

WHEREAS, a Certificate of the Register of the Land Office at THE DALLES, OREGON,

has been deposited in the General Land Office, whereby it appears that, pursuant to the Act of Congress of May 20, 1862,

"To Secure Homesteads to Actual Settlers on the Public Domain," and the acts supplemental thereto, the claim of

LEWIS R. WILSON

has been established and duly consummated, in conformity to law, for the SOUTHWEST QUARTER OF SECTION FOUR

IN TOWNSHIP EIGHTEEN SOUTH OF RANGE SIXTEEN EAST OF THE WILLAMETTE MERIDIAN,

OREGON, CONTAINING ONE HUNDRED SIXTY ACRES,

according to the Official Plat of the Survey of the said Land, returned to the GENERAL LAND OFFICE by the Surveyor-General:

NOW KNOW YE, That there is, therefore, granted by the UNITED STATES unto the said claimant   the tract of Land above described;
TO HAVE AND TO HOLD the said tract of Land, with the appurtenances thereof, unto the said claimant   and to the heirs and assigns of
the said claimant   forever; subject to any vested and accrued water rights for mining, agricultural, manufacturing, or other purposes, and
rights to ditches and reservoirs used in connection with such water rights, as may be recognized and acknowledged by the local customs, laws,
and decisions of courts; and there is reserved from the lands hereby granted, a right of way thereon for ditches or canals constructed by the
authority of the United States.

IN TESTIMONY WHEREOF, I,   WILLIAM H. TAFT

President of the United States of America, have caused these letters to be made

Patent, and the seal of the General Land Office to be hereunto affixed.

GIVEN under my hand, at the City of Washington, the   EIGHTH

(SEAL)   day of   APRIL   in the year of our Lord one thousand

nine hundred and   ELEVEN   and of the Independence of the

.../Image_Conversion.asp?Accession=188758&Format=SmallGIF&Page=1&QryID=52175%2E136/1/04

Document of homestead property

Appendix 187

Widow's Name Taken From Petition to Set Aside L. R. Wilson Will

At her own request Mrs. Emma Wilson, widow of the late Lewis R. Wilson of Halsey, has withdrawn her name from the list of petitioners who are contesting Mr. Wilson's will. The order permitting her to withdraw was signed late yesterday by County Judge D. O. Woodworth, who ruled that the act would abridge "no substantial right of the petitioners."

Some of the children of the deceased are attacking the will, which left most of the property to Mrs. Lily Curtis, a daughter, on the ground that it was not the true last will and testament of the deceased.

Emma doesn't contest Lewis' will

REDMOND, OREGON, 9-28-1931

Mr Lewis C Wilson
Shedd Oregon

Rmond L. Jones, M. D.

FOR PROFESSIONAL SERVICES

Ambulance (Mr Cliff Ralston)	55 00
Trip to Portland from Redmond Ore (180 miles) and assistance at operation on Mrs Wilson for acute appendicitis	200 00

RECEIVED PAYMENT

Raymond F Jones MD

Bill paid by check on Halsey State Bank by Mrs Lilly W. Clutter

*Drs. order to transport Emma Wilson from Prineville
to Portland hospital due to appendicitis 1931*

To ROBERT MONTGOMERY and C.W.WILSON:

YOU ARE HEREBY NOTIFIED to deliver up the possession of the land now occupied by you and belonging to me, and more particularly described as the Northwest quarter (N.W.¼) of Section Twenty-two (22) in Township Fourteen (14) South, Range Four (4) West of the Willamette Meridian, in Linn County, Oregon, on or before the 1st.day of October, 1928.

AND YOU ARE HEREBY NOTIFIED that if you do not give possession on or before said date that I will commence proceedings to oust you therefrom.

I also expect you to pay the rent due thereon before said date.

DATED this 22d.day of May, 1928.

Eviction Notice to Clarence Wilson from Lewis Wilson

Miss Wilson, Pioneer Teacher, Dies in Portland

Miss Adwilda Wilson, who taught the first public school in Redmond in the old hardware building in 1907, died October 1 in Portland, where she had made her home since 1935.

Funeral services were held Monday at Finley's rose chapel in Portland, and commitment was in Pine Grove cemetery, Halsey.

When she taught in Redmond she gave a school program to raise the money to buy the first school bell, her sister, Mrs. L. A. McFadden, recalled. The unexpected highlight of the program came when the butterfly costume of one of the young performers caught fire from the lamps but did not hurt the child.

Miss Wilson came to Oregon in 1885 and lived near Halsey until 1907 when she came to central Oregon. She taught in Culver and Prineville until 1912, when she moved to Albany and taught there until 1928.

She is survived by three sisters, Mrs. L. A. McFadden of Redmond, Miss Abbie Wilson and Mrs. Lillie W. Curtis. Mrs. McFadden returned to Redmond Tuesday after attending the funeral.

JOHN BERT BREED
430 E. 98th St., Inglewood
Services Monday 10 a.m. Chapel of the Chimes, Inglewood Park Cemetery. Dunaway-Fox, Hawthorne, directors.

SANTA CLAUS

...ke
...ip

I Kroger store ...ed one of "men" have already attracted a large number of Beardstownians and others.

John N. Janes, clock company head, originated the unique display, for entry in the Philadelphia Hobby show, which he attended and where the rig caught the eye of hundreds of thousands.

Mr. Janes calls the performers "do dos" and has manufactured and packaged thousands of the smaller toys for the children—the display in the window, of course, is much larger than the toys manufactured by the International Toy and Hobby Company.

Operated through the use of a one quarter horse power motor and an intricate system of cables, wires and pulleys, the display is "turned on" at 11 o'clock every morning and kept in operation until midnight.

Mr. Janes says he contemplates operating the display through the Christmas season for the delight of the children.

Also on display in the window are the famous Middlebury Whip Kings—said by Mr. Janes to be the best mixers on the market.

Janes' Trapeze Performers Attract Hundreds to Display

The Whip King, the Copper Clock, and the Four Leaf Clover clock were among the manufactured articles Mr. Janes displayed at Philadelphia in Convention Hall in November.

---

fell from 84 to 76 cents during this period.

A spokesman of the AMI's department of marketing at San Francisco predicted an increase in meat production next year, most of it during the last quarter of 1949 and in 1950. He said retail meat prices declined 12 per cent since early fall.

Meanwhile, a large food chain (National Tea Co.) announced an eight to 10 cent cut in the price of steaks and beef roasts. A com-

---

Services To Be ...stry Saturday

...al services for John B ... 85. Industry resta... will be held at 1:30 ... at the Clugston Fu... in Industry. Burial wi... stry Cemetery. He ... dead in bed at his

...as born March 25, 18... William D. and Mary David ... on a farm west of Industry. ... young man he was employe... the old Jacksonville Easte... road.

In 1893 he started a re... in Casper, Wyo., and too... homestead there. From C... returned to Adair, where ... ed a restaurant. Later he... to Macomb and operated ... taurant, then moved to ... land, where he operated ... restaurants. He lived ... Island about 20 years.

In 1917 he retired and m... Industry, and later re-ent... restaurant business which ... erated until his death. At ... he had a restaurant in Bea... two years.

He was a life member ... Brotherhood of Locomoti... men and Engineers. He ... member of Consistory at ... land.

On June 2, 1893 he ... Blanche G. Merrick, w... Jan. 18, 1950. Surviving ... daughter, Mrs. Beatrice ... Idaho Springs, Colo.; a s... M. Janes of Beardstown; ... son; a granddaughter, ... sisters, Mrs. Blanche ... Mrs. Lucy McDonald a... Ruth Hines, all of Los ... Calif., Mrs. Nina Eades o... and Mrs. Sadie Scott of ... Falls, Tex.

Friends may call at the ... home after 6 p.m. Thurs...

Adwilda Wilson and Blanche husband history

: I94496516
me: Thomas WATSON
en Name: Thomas
name: Watson
: M
th: 14 Jul 1826 in Ireland
ath: 24 Jul 1907 in Oxford,IA
te:

ACCORDING TO HIS OBITUARY, THOMAS WATSON WAS BORN ON JULY 14, 1826 IN IRELAND. HE CAME TO THE UNITED STATES WHEN HE WAS 17 YEARS OLD, STOPPING FIRST AT PHILADELPHIA BEFORE COMING ON TO NEW YORK. REGUARDING HIS CHILDHOOD WE CAN ONLY SURMISE THAT BEING SCOTCH-IRISH HE WAS BROUGHT UP ON THE PRINCIPLES OF HONEST WORK AND FRUGALITY, AND THAT HE WAS FORTUNATE TO HAVE LEFT IRELAND PRIOR TO THE BEGINNING OF THE POTATO FAMINE. HOW THOMAS , HIS BROTHERS AND THE GIRLS THEY MARRIED FOUND THEIR WAY TO THE RURAL COMMUNITIES NORTH OF NEW YORK CITY WE DO NOT KNOW. LIKE HIS BROTHER , WILLIAM THE FIRST ACTUAL RECORD WE HAVE OF HIM IS IN THIS COUNTRY IS THE CENSUS OF 1850 FOR CARMEL IN PUTNAM COUNTY. HERE HE IS SHOWN TO BE 24 YEARS OLD AND HIS OCCUPATION IS LISTED AS "LABORER"

MARY ANN'S OBITUARY STATES THAT SHE WAS BORN IN KAVANAUGH IRELAND ON MARCH 30, 1835. SHE CAME TO AMERICA AT THE AGE OF FIFTEEN (CA1850) WAS CONVERTED AND JOINED THE METHODIST CHURCH WHEN SHE WAS A YOUNG WOMEN, AFTER SHE HAD COME TO THE U.S. FAMILY TRADITION HAS IT THAT MARY ANN WAS RELATED TO THE ENGLISH GENERAL HOWE "AND WAS PROUD OF IT." IT ALSO IS SAID THAT HER MOTHER DIED ON THE SHIP COMING OVER, BUT NO TRACE OF OTHER RELATIVES HAS BEEN FOUND.

ACCORDING TO THE FAMILY BIBLE, THOMAS AND MARY ANN WERE MARRIED ON THE 13TH OF FEBRUARY, 1856. HE WOULD HAVE BEEN 30 AND SHE 21. ALSO RECORDED ARE THE BIRTHS OF THEIR NINE CHILDREN AND THE DEATHS OF THE THREE THAT DIED YOUNG. SOON AFTER THEIR MARRIAGE IN PUTNAM COUNTY, THOMAS AND MARY ANN MOVED TO ILLINOIS. BY THE RAILROADS HAD PUSHED AS FAR WEST AS THE MISSISSIPPI RIVER, AND IT IS REASONABLE TO ASSUME THAT THE TRIP FROM NEW YORK TO ILLINOIS WAS MADE BY RAIL. ALSO, ON THE BASIS OF SKIMPY, BUT LOGICAL INDICATIONS, IT IS THOUGHT THAT THE TWO BROTHERS, THOMAS AND WILLIAM, MAY HAVE COME WEST TOGETHER.

Information on Thomas and Mary Ann Watson

Lilly having fun

BIOGRAPHIES

TONI GILBERT, MA

The author, Toni Gilbert, is the granddaughter of Ellsworth and Lilly Wilson Curtis, subjects in this family history. Many hours of Ms. Gilbert's youth were spent beside Lilly Wilson Curtis, at the kitchen sink and at the old treadle sewing machine, listening as her grandmother passed on her knowledge and her life skills.

Today, a transpersonal counselor with a background in holistic nursing, Ms. Gilbert holds an associate's degree in nursing and a bachelor's degree in psychology and art. She pursued her interest in art and its symbolism in a graduate art therapy program and earned a master's degree from the Institute of Transpersonal Psychology.

Ms. Gilbert's first book, *Messages from the Archetypes: Using Tarot for Healing and Spiritual Growth*, is published by White Cloud Press. Her second book, *Gaining Archetypal Vision*, is published by Schiffer Books. To read articles Ms. Gilbert has published both locally and nationally, visit www.tonigilbert.com.

In the recent past, Ms. Gilbert worked in the field of mental-health nursing and owned Centre of Main St., a wellness center in Jefferson, Oregon, where she saw clients and facilitated therapeutic groups. In addition, she has taught psychology at two community colleges. More recently, Ms. Gilbert established the Northwest Astrology & Tarot Salon, www.nwsalon.com; was the founding editor of the *Alternative Journal of Nursing*; the founding director of the *Oregon Holistic Nurses Association*, www.oregonholisticnurses. org; founder of the Jefferson Historic Society & Museum in Jefferson, Oregon.

LYLE CURTIS, CONTRIBUTOR

Lyle Curtis, contributor to this book, is the grandson of Ellsworth and Lilly Wilson Curtis. He grew to adulthood near Logsden, Oregon. After completing his tour of duty in the U.S. Air Force, he worked for the Oregon Department of Fish and Wildlife. In 1986, Mr. Curtis contributed to the *Fish Hatchery Ways and Means Manual,* which was distributed at conferences for the Department of Fish and Wildlife and to fish hatcheries across the state.

After living at Rose Lodge for five years, Mr. Curtis moved back to the site of a log-house home of his childhood on the Siletz River, where he currently resides, in a newer home, with his wife, Kathy Curtis. There, they raise a few cattle, have a small flock of chickens, and follow the ageless custom, of growing a good-sized garden each year.

Now retired, Mr. Curtis continues his research into the lives of his ancestors, both on-line and in person, and has traveled to the eastern and southern United States, to Iowa, and to Illinois, seeking further information about the lineage of the Curtis and Wilson families.

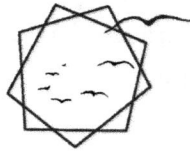